Language Lessons *for* Children

by Kathy Weitz

Primer Two

Teaching Helps

for Autumn, Winter, & Spring

PREFACE

When I began educating my children at home more than two decades ago, one of the first books I read was *For the Children's Sake* by Susan Schaeffer Macaulay. Here I was formally introduced to the philosophies of Charlotte Mason, a Victorian education reformer. In my girlhood, L. M. Montgomery had given me a first glimpse of similar methods via *Anne of Avonlea*, so Charlotte Mason's ideas immediately attracted me. Later, I read her complete series on education which provided additional insight and encouragement. After all these years and after teaching many students of all ages (my own and others), I continue to consider many of her methods ideal for teaching young children and the perfect preparation for a rigorous classical education later.

All of the ideas and methods contained in the *Language Lessons for Children* series have been field tested and honed in several educational settings with students of differing ages, abilities, and learning styles. The primary testers have been my own five sons and one daughter in our homeschool classroom.

Language Lessons for Children is a work of "heart". It is the series I wish I had had when my children were young. It is the result of much trial and error on my part. I pray that it will provide structure, simplicity, and much delight for those tasked with the instruction of young students in our extraordinary English language.

~kpw
Soli Deo Gloria!
April, 2014

Acknowledgements

Although my name is on the cover, the Primer series in many ways has been a collaborative effort. I owe a great debt of gratitude to many folks. The gorgeous cover designs are the craftsmanship of my friend Jayme Metzgar, with image credit to The Graphics Fairy (www.thegraphicsfairy.com). Many other friends have helped with both editing and content: in particular, Kimberlynn Curles, Emily Cook, Cheryl Turner, Karen Gill, Carolyn Vance, Lene Jaqua, and the exceptional teachers, moms, and students of Providence Preparatory Academy. And of course, the main source of help and encouragement in myriad ways—from design consultation to field testing to dinner duty—has come from my dear husband and my wonderful children.

~kpw

Primer Two Teaching Helps
CONTENTS

Primer Two Spring Teaching Helps & Notes

Appendix

INTRODUCTION

My heart overflows with a pleasing theme;
I address my verses to the king;
my tongue is like the pen of a ready scribe.
~ Psalm 45:1, ESV

All Language Lessons at Cottage Press aim to develop *ready scribes* who pen *pleasing themes* flowing from a heart of truth, goodness, and beauty. The *Primer* series is designed to provide gentle yet meaningful lessons for early elementary students in preparation for more rigorous grammar and composition instruction in late elementary, middle, and high school.

Weekly copybook and narration selections are drawn from classic children's literature and poetry. These time-proven imitation methods fill students' minds with a ready supply of elegant and beautiful words and patterns of expression, and equip their imaginations with a delightful treasury of stories. Nature and art study lessons included each week also provide "scope for the imagination", and hone the students' powers of observation, description, and attention to detail—necessary attributes for *ready scribes*.

Primer books are sequential in skills: *Primer One Autumn, Primer One Winter,* and *Primer One Spring* followed by *Primer Two Autumn, Primer Two Winter,* and *Primer Two Spring.* Familiarity with the concepts from the preceding book is assumed, but the lessons are so straightforward that students may begin at their current skill level.

Students beginning *Primer One* should have achieved

beginning spelling and phonics proficiency, be ready for beginning chapter books, and be able to copy words and sentences. Students beginning *Primer Two* should have achieved intermediate spelling and phonics proficiency, be able to read beginning chapter books with basic fluency, and be able to copy sentences and short paragraphs. *Primer One* is very generally appropriate for 2nd to 3rd grade students, and *Primer Two* for 3rd to 4th grade students, but both could be used very effectively by older students as well.

ℭℜ Lesson Format

Each *Primer* book is divided into twelve weeks of study. Each week is divided into four days' work, with a poetry or prose selection at its heart. Each day's lesson includes a short copybook exercise from the copybook selection and a brief grammar or phonics review exercise connected with the copybook selection. The weekly routine also includes narration exercises on Days 1 and 3, a nature study lesson on Day 2, and a picture study lesson on Day 4. Detailed directions for each of these lesson components is provided in the Pedagogy & Practice section below.

ℭℜ Lesson Preparation

The lessons in this book are designed to free teachers from as much preparation work as possible. For the most part, you will just open to the week's lesson and begin. Additional preparation may be necessary if you opt to add the enrichment ideas included *Teaching Helps*, but even that preparation is minimal.

PEDAGOGY & PRACTICE

৭ COPYBOOK

The method is simple: students copy a worthy copybook selection—a poem, a psalm, a hymn, or a prose passage. They carefully reproduce the text of the copybook selection in their best handwriting with proper spelling, punctuation, and capitalization. In *Primer One*, space is provided in the student workbook for each copybook assignment. In *Primer Two*, students complete copybook assignments in a separate composition book dedicated to the purpose.

Copybook sessions should be no longer than ten minutes for most students. Some students will need even shorter sessions in the beginning. If necessary, divide the copybook selection into several parts and complete the work over two or three sessions during the day. It is better to complete only a portion of the copybook selection in an excellent manner than to slog through the entire thing in a sloppy manner. If a student really struggles, begin by requiring only a single sentence. Require an incremental amount more in each subsequent lesson until the student is able to complete the entire selection in one sitting.

Before students begin copying, spend a few minutes together reading and examining the copybook selection. Point out the punctuation and capitalization. Discuss any words that might be difficult to spell. Instruct students to use their best handwriting and to copy each letter and punctuation mark accurately.

At the end of each copybook session, have students compare

what they have written with the original. If they have made mistakes and do not catch them this way, go through the copybook selection with them word by word. Is each word spelled correctly? Is each capital letter and punctuation mark reproduced correctly? If need be, go letter by letter through words they have misspelled. This process may seem tedious, but it will prove invaluable to students trained by it to catch their own mistakes. Some students will need help to focus on specific and small details continuously. Do not hesitate to give students this kind of help. Independence will come eventually as they consistently practice a habit of attention to detail.

A NOTE ABOUT POETRY COPYBOOK ~ For poetry copybook selections, have students align the verses to the left, since it is difficult to center handwritten lines. The daily copybook selections are left-aligned for this reason. In *Primer One*, poems at the beginning of a week are centered for aesthetic reasons.

A NOTE ABOUT SCRIPTURE COPYBOOK SELECTIONS ~ *Primer* copybook selections are taken from the New King James version of the Bible. In general, the King James version is preferable for language lessons because of its incomparable language patterns and expressiveness. Familiarity with the King James style is vital for our students because so many important literary, theological, and political works employ this style. However, because the *Primer* student is still learning basic spelling, grammar, and word usage conventions, it is prudent to offer the New King James version for this level. The New King James retains much of the beauty and form of the King James, but updates the verb and pronoun forms, along with other grammar features.

A NOTE ABOUT NAMES REFERRING TO THE TRINITY ~ *Primer* copybook selections follow the convention of capitalizing pronouns that refer to the persons of the Trinity. Some translators and theologians do not follow this convention, so if you prefer that students not capitalize these words, just make the change in the text.

ℭ DICTATION

On Day 4 of each week, students write a portion of the copybook selection from dictation. For students who are new to both copybook and dictation, do a bit of both. Start by dictating a single sentence, then have students copy another sentence or two.

Allow students to study the copybook selection before you begin to dictate. Point out capitalization and punctuation features. Go over the spelling of any words that could give trouble. You may even give hints reminding students of the capitalization, punctuation, and spelling details as you dictate. Tell students exactly what they need to know at each word, each punctuation mark. Spell difficult words on the board where they can see them.

Gradually increase the length of the dictation selection and decrease the number of helps and hints you give. As students advance, adjust the challenge level by increasing the speed of dictation and decreasing the number of repetitions you give.

Students should eventually be able to take dictation without any help or hints, but this takes time and patience. Some students will be faster at achieving this goal than others.

Do not worry if students continue to need help through this series.

ᴄᴙ Spelling, Grammar, and Word Usage

Lessons on most days include a short spelling or grammar exercise drawn from the daily copybook. This is intended to supplement, not replace, the students' other phonics and spelling studies. The importance of systematic and thorough phonics instruction in the elementary years cannot be overstated. My own preferred approach for phonics instruction is that which Romalda Spalding developed in *The Writing Road for Reading*. There are several excellent curricula available based on this approach. See the *Primer Resources Webpage* for links to suggested resources.

The majority of these lessons are self-explanatory, but notes and answer keys are provided in the following pages as the activities warrant.

Whenever students are instructed to write or copy words, have them read back to you what they have written, *exactly* as written. Have them make corrections as needed at this point. This is a very important step for students, as it both reinforces correct spelling and promotes editing skills.

As the exercises become more difficult, do not hesitate to help students and even give them answers if they struggle. Keep in mind that this is an introduction to many concepts, and some students will need much practice before these things become automatic. In particular, do help them with homonyms, synonyms, and antonyms, as some of the words needed for answers may be completely new to students.

CR READING AND NARRATION

Twice a week, you will read a short fable or narrative with students, and they will narrate it back to you. The ability to clearly articulate a story is a foundational skill required for virtually every type of writing: essays, research reports, legal documents. Students must learn to recall a story sequentially as well as discern its most important parts. Many children are natural storytellers and enjoy this greatly. You will need access to the classic children's book from which the narratives for each *Primer* are drawn. See the Required Materials section in each *Primer* for the book needed to accomapny the particular workbook you are using.

Narration is meant to be a simple process. Prepare students for the copybook selection by reviewing the listed vocabulary words and explaining the meanings as needed in very simple terms.

For younger students, read the narrative aloud, then ask them to tell you the story. Many students will need no prompting at all. Some students may need a bit of help getting started. For example, you may write on the board the names of the main characters in order of appearance as a subtle reminder of the sequence. The vocabulary words may also be helpful for this purpose.

Students who are advancing in their reading skills may be able to read all or part of the copybook selection aloud to you. For these students, it is still best to alternate the initial reading method. Read one day's selection to them, then allow them to read the next day's selection on their own so that they gain practice in listening as well as reading skills regularly.

The best way to teach students to narrate is to model it yourself. Read a story aloud and narrate it to them afterwards. This will help you to see the challenges they will face in narration. You may even find that this is a skill you need to work on.

After students have narrated back to you orally, they may draw a picture or a series of pictures in the space provided to illustrate the story.

☙ NATURE STUDY

Regular nature walks with students are a must. Give your young students plenty of opportunity for first-hand observation and tactile experience with the natural world. Fresh air, sunshine, and exercise for all of you are the healthy side benefits.

Nature study at this age should rely mostly on the student's own observations, but if your physical location makes that difficult or impossible, you may also need to pick up some books from the library or use online resources.

The nature study exercises are fairly self-explanatory. Students observe, draw, or collect (if possible) a nature specimen from your yard or a nearby park. Notes on each week's nature study lesson are provided in the *Teaching Notes and Helps* section of this book. In some cases you will read a short selection from this section to students and/or view resources at the *Primer Resources Webpage*, linked from the Cottage Press website, *cottagepress.net*.

Keep nature study brief and simple. Delighting in God's creation is as much a goal of nature study as learning to identify and classify. When you go on a nature walk, take along a sketch pad. Make quick sketches and notes of what you observe. Bring back specimens if at all possible, so students can take their time for a more complete and careful drawing.

Start a collection of field guides, and bookmark helpful websites for nature identification. The *Primer Resources Webpage* has links to websites and resources to get you started.

ॐ Picture Study

Picture study sharpens students' powers of observation. It forms a sense of beauty. It teaches students discernment and appreciation of true quality in art. Students study each artist's work for a period of six weeks, in order that they may become familiar with that artist's particular style.

Choose two artists to accompany each *Primer* book. You will need to print out the six works by each artist you have chosen. Cottage Press provides free downloadable PDF documents for a variety of well-known artists whose works will appeal to younger students. Each picture is copyrighted, as per the person or museum who owns it. These cannot be sold as a printed book, but the copyright allows for you to print them in the size you need.

Each Picture Study PDF also provides you with a few biographical notes on the artists that you may mention to students. However, the primary goal at this age is for the students to observe and describe.

Allow students a few minutes to quietly observe the painting. Tell them to try to remember as many details as possible. Then hide the picture and ask them to tell you what they saw. You may need to offer a little help to get them started: "There was a big cow in the center of the picture. What surrounded it?" Do not explain the picture to them. Give just enough help that they can take over on their own. They may want to describe the picture orally or in writing, or they may want to sketch it from memory.

Many students will need a little practice to do this well. In a classroom or co-op setting, allow the youngest students to go first, and then ask the others to give additional details. Students quickly realize that they must look for lots of details so that they will have something to add. If you are working one-on-one with a student, you may need to help by taking turns describing one detail each. As in the narration exercises, model the process of observation and description.

Below are a few questions you can use as prompts. These begin to introduce some art terminology in a gentle and natural manner that actually makes the task of description easier.

• What part of the picture is your eye immediately drawn towards?
• How did the artist draw your eye there?
• What do you see in the foreground?
• What do you see in the background?

• Where is the light coming from in this picture? (*Observe the shadows and light spots.*)

After students have observed and described the painting, have them do their best to reproduce it in the space provided using high-quality colored pencils. Alternately, you can print out the picture and have them cut and paste it in the space. A few blank lines are included at the bottom of each picture study page. Students should copy the title of the picture and the name of the artist with the year the artwork was produced.

See links to resources for further study at the *Primer Resources Webpage*. Find books about the artist you are studying. Look for additional works by the artist. Check to see if your local art museum has any of the artist's works in its gallery.

Weekly Routine

"Habit is either the best of servants or the worst of masters." ~ Nathanael Emmons

Routine (habit) is one of the most important things to establish in students' schoolwork, and extremely beneficial to them in every area of life. Charlotte Mason often likened habits to train tracks that allow a child's life to run smoothly and evenly through the day. Her thoughts on this apply to both home life and school life:

> *"The mother who takes pains to endow her children with good habits secures for herself smooth and easy days; While she who lets their habits take care of themselves has a weary life of endless friction with the children."*
>
> ~ Charlotte Mason, *Home Education*, p. 136

Young children thrive when they know what to expect next; the daily routine or order of schoolwork creates an environment that optimizes learning.

An important habit for children to devlop is the that of paying careful attention to what they are doing. Short lessons at this age make this habit much easier for all children to learn. Consider moving to a different kind of activity between each section of the daily lessons. For example, just after completing copybook, have students do some kind of physical motion—even if it is just getting up and stretching or sharpening their pencils. Particularly after any part of the lesson that requires strong concentration and close eye focus, try to incorporate a short physical activity.

Cʒ SAMPLE LESSON PLAN

Here is a suggested order for completing the daily work in *Language Lessons for Children Primers.*

1. Begin each day's session with students by reading the weekly selection aloud. Make sure you read with proper pauses and with feeling and expression. On the first day of a new lesson, talk with students about the copybook selection and make sure they understand it. On subsequent days, continue to read the copybook selection aloud to students, and then have them read it to you. Set a goal to have the students read with good feeling and expression by the end of the week. Encourage students to memorize the copybook selection. Each week's selection has a drawing page opposite. Have students illustrate the copybook selection on this page at some point during the week.

2. Have students write the date in the "Today is..." section. As they are learning how to do this, write the date out for them to copy. Use this format:

   Monday, October 3, 2014

3. Go over the day's copybook selection with students as detailed in Pedagogy and Practice above. At first, students may need you to sit with them as they complete their work. Do this as long as necessary, but work towards more independence in completing lessons over time. Copybook sessions should be short (five to ten minutes). If necessary, complete this over several copybook sessions in one day. Have students check their work at the end of each session.

4. Help students complete the spelling or grammar lesson accurately.

5. Do the reading and narration, picture study, or nature study lesson.

It is worth repeating: keep lessons short and varied. Avoid having young children complete all of this work in one long sitting. Here is an example of how I might structure Day 2 for my eight-year-old son at home.

- Read weekly selection together.
- Complete about half of the copybook selection and check it.
- Feed the cat.
- Review the spelling or grammar lesson; complete and check.
- Go over the vocabulary for the narration lesson.
- Get up and do a little bit of stretching or run around the outside of the house three times.
- Move to the sofa to do the reading and narration lesson.
- Enjoy a snack.
- Complete the rest of the copybook selection and check it.

Of course, your particulars will vary. Some students will be able to sit and focus for longer periods of time, but I have found that most students, particularly boys, do best with this kind of routine.

Optional Enrichment Ideas

℞ MEMORIZE THE WEEKLY SELECTION Try to schedule a recitation before an audience periodically. Parents, grandparents, siblings, and friends generally make an encouraging audience, as do residents of a local elder care facility. Recitation is wonderful preparation for public speaking.

℞ READ THE WHOLE BOOK If the copybook selection comes from a longer book or story, try to read the entire story at some point during the week.

℞ READ MORE BOOKS Find books on your shelf or at the library that give more information on the nature topic for the week. Look for books with lots of pictures and illustrations. Also check the *1000 Good Books* list, which suggests books for read alouds for every age group:

www.classical-homeschooling.org/celoop/1000.html

℞ PLAN A FIELD TRIP to a local art gallery, zoo, arboretum, nature preserve, or observatory.

A Note to Home Educating Parents[1]

"Richer than I you can never be-
I had a Mother who read to me."
~ Strickland Gillilan

Read, read, read to your child! I cannot emphasize this strongly enough. Take it from a mom of grown children—this is a fleeting opportunity, so treasure the time reading with your child. And keep reading to your child even as he reaches the teen and young adult years. The ideas, characters, and language in the books you read together will become part of the 'language' of your family and give you countless opportunities for discussion.

Do not allow busy schedules to crowd out this vital component of developing the soul of your child. Prioritize reading with your child above co-ops, enrichment classes, and even sports. It is one of the best investments you can make in your child's education, as well as in your relationship with him. Make reading aloud a routine in your homeschool and in your daily life with your child. Guard this time with your life.

Select worthy books with lovely illustrations. Choose books both you and your child will enjoy, and do not forget to reread favorites. There are so many marvelous classic children's books. Do not waste time reading 'twaddle'—books that are shallow and condescending to children, as unfortunately many children's books are. Be discerning in your choices. Just as setting healthy eating patterns early

1 This note is excerpted from a talk entitled Joy in the Homeschool Journey which I have given to several local homeschool groups.

in life can create lifelong healthy habits, so establishing a taste for worthy books in his early years can help train his appetite for great books in later years.

Horace E. Scudder, the late nineteenth century editor of The Atlantic Monthly and compiler of great literature for children wrote, "There is no academy on earth equal to a mother's reading to her child." I could not agree more.

Primer Two Autumn Teaching Helps & Notes

The Land of Story-Books

At evening when the lamp is lit,
Around the fire my parents sit;
They sit at home and talk and sing,
And do not play at anything.

Now, with my little gun, I crawl
All in the dark along the wall,
And follow round the forest track
Away behind the sofa back.

There, in the night, where none can spy,
All in my hunter's camp I lie,
And play at books that I have read
Till it is time to go to bed.

These are the hills, these are the woods,
These are my starry solitudes;
And there the river by whose brink
The roaring lions come to drink.

I see the others far away
As if in firelit camp they lay,
And I, like to an Indian scout,
Around their party prowled about.

So, when my nurse comes in for me,
Home I return across the sea,
And go to bed with backward looks
At my dear land of Story-books.

~ Robert Louis Stevenson

ℭ Copybook & Dictation

Note that the first letter of each line of poetry is capitalized.

CR Spelling, Grammar, & Word Usage

Do not hesitate to help students and prompt them with answers if they struggle. The Primers provide a simple introduction to grammar concepts and proper word usage, but most students will need much practice with them.

Day 1 *Plurals* Note that this discussion of making words plural refers only to words that name persons, places, things, or ideas (nouns). Nouns, along with other parts of speech, are introduced beginning in *Primer Two,* Week 3.

Review with students which words use **-es** when making plurals. Remind them that they need to listen the the end of the root word. If it ends in **/ch/**, **/sh/**, **/x/**, **/s/**, and **/z/**, it will probably require an **-es**. If the root word 'hisses' add **-es**. Help students identify the two sounds you hear in the consonant **x** (k + s).

Plurals: lamps, fires, parents, tracks, woods, parties, stories, churches, boxes

Day 2 *Days of the Week & Abbreviations* The concept of "think to spell" is a way for students to learn correct spelling of words with unusual letter combinations or silent letters like the days of the week or the months of the year. Pronounce the word the way it is spelled, emphasizing the silent or unusual letters within the word. Use this method with *Tuesday* (Tu · ES · day) and *Wednesday* (Wed · NES · day). "Think to spell" will not always correspond to proper syllabication, as in the word *Tuesday*, which the dictionary divides *Tues · day*. When proper syllabication is needed, the dictionary is the final authority.

Days of the week and months of the year are abbreviated in different ways. Teach the simplest form (first three letters followed by a period), but show students the other ways as well. Sometimes Tuesday and Thursday will use four or five letters followed by a period (Tues., Thurs.) Days of the week can also be abbreviated with just one or two capital letters and no period (M, TU, W, TH, F, SA, SU). Months can be abbreviated with just three capital letters (JAN, FEB, MAR, APR, MAY, JUN, JUL, AUG, SEP, OCT, NOV, DEC). Why does May have no abbreviation? (*Only three letters!*)

Day 3 *Rhyming Words*
Have students replace the beginning consonant(s) with different single letter and letter blends. Refer to the list of beginning blends in the Appendix of *Teaching Helps*. Help students spell the rhyming words correctly, since they may differ from the spelling pattern of the original. If you need help, use a rhyming dictionary or online rhyming source.

Rhyming Words (will vary): day, clay, stay, pray, neigh, yea; lamp, stamp, champ

Words that rhyme with time: grime, lime, rhyme, climb

Remind students to begin sentences with a capital letter and end with end punctuation.

℞ NATURE STUDY[1]
Finding Direction Even in this age of Google Maps and GPS devices, a good sense of direction is a basic skill everyone needs to develop. It is really a safety precaution,

---

1 Before beginning *Nature Study* this week, secure a digital or hard copy of Home Geography. See the *Materials Required* list in the front of *Primer One Autumn*.

particularly valuable when young people begin to drive.

In *Primer One Autumn*, students were introduced to the concept of direction in the context of their immediate surroundings using the mnemonic **N**ever **E**at **S**hredded **W**heat.

Read these lessons from *Home Geography* with students, and complete the oral exercises.

- ✓ Lesson I: Position
- ✓ Lesson II: How the Sun Shows Direction
- ✓ Lesson IV: How the Compass Shows Direction
- ✓ Lesson V: Questions on Direction (skip the questions related to stars)

For now, skip Lesson III: How the Stars Show Direction. We will come back to this in *Primer Two Winter*.

Study some maps with students before they draw their picture maps. Note how the compass rose is used. The *Primer* Resources Webpage contains links to sites that will help you teach students to find direction with and without a compass. You can find many enrichment activities on these sites. This could be a fun field day activity.

AUTUMN, WEEK 2

from EARLY DAYS IN EGYPT

In the valley of the river Nile, bathed in glittering sunshine, lay the ancient land of Egypt, a narrow strip of green in the midst of the sands of the desert.

From the tall mountains of Central Africa, the Nile cut its way between tall cliffs that glowed rose-pink and lilac, flecked with passing shadows, and lifting clear cut outlines against a bright blue sky.

Six times the river, flowing down on its long way to the sea, halted in its course to swirl in foaming cataracts around obstructing rocks, jagged heaps of black granite, that lay as though hurled by giants across the bed of the stream.

~ Olive Beaupre-Miller, A Picturesque Tale of Progress, Volume I

ଔ COPYBOOK & DICTATION

The first word of each paragraph of prose is indented. In typeset, you will sometimes see paragraphs that are not indented when they are separated by a line, as in this book. Students should always indent when writing by hand.

ଔ SPELLING, GRAMMAR, & WORD USAGE

Day 1 *Past Tense*

Past Tense: cut, glittered, glowed, lifted, flowed, halted, swirled, hurled, was

Day 2 *Homonyms*

Learning to spell and use homonyms correctly will help students avoid many common spelling errors. When students write homonyms, have them use each one in a sentence orally to make sure they know which spelling to use in context. Give students plenty of help with these exercises.

Homonyms: son, rows, blew, weigh and whey, two and too, see

Day 3 *Synonyms*

Synonyms (will vary): antique, old, bygone; sliced, gashed, carved; high, soaring; shone, blazed, flamed; stopped; threw, tossed, pitched

Day 4 *Plurals* The word *valley* ends with a **-y**; but this word does not change the **y** to an **i** and add **-es**. The "**y** changing" rule only applies when the **y** is a single vowel, and not a vowel digraph as in **monkey, play,** and **toy.** This rule also only applies if you are adding a suffix which begins with a vowel. Refer back to your phonics or spelling program if you need additional help in reviewing this concept.

Plurals: valleys, strips, deserts, mountains, cliffs, shadows, cataracts, joys, ways

ʕ NATURE STUDY
Drawing Plans Introduce this lesson with *Home Geography* lessons:

✓ Lesson VIII: Pictures and Plans

✓ Lesson IX: Written Exercise

Lesson VII: How to Tell Distance is optional. If you teach this lesson, you may require students to use accurate measurements in their drawings. Otherwise, just help students to make the objects in the drawings roughly proportional.

AUTUMN, WEEK 3

from PSALM 27

[1]The Lord is my light and my salvation—
whom shall I fear?

The Lord is the stronghold of my life—
of whom shall I be afraid?

[2] When the wicked advance against me
to devour me,
it is my enemies and my foes
who will stumble and fall.
[3] Though an army besiege me,
my heart will not fear;
though war break out against me,
even then I will be confident.

[4] One thing I ask from the Lord,
this only do I seek:
that I may dwell in the house of the Lord
all the days of my life,
to gaze on the beauty of the Lord
and to seek him in his temple.
[5] For in the day of trouble
he will keep me safe in his dwelling;
he will hide me in the shelter of his sacred tent
and set me high upon a rock.

~ Psalm 27:1-5, New King James Version

⚭ COPYBOOK & DICTATION

See *A Note About Scripture Copybook Selections* and *A Note About Names Referring to the Trinity* in the Copybook section of Pedagogy and Practice.

It is not necessary for students to copy the verse numbers, but they may do so if you or they prefer. Discuss this with them, and give them direction as to how they should note the verse number if you choose to do so (as a superscript, in parentheses, or preceded by a lowercase **v** followed by a period).

ℛ Spelling, Grammar, & Word Usage

Day 1 *The Noun* Give students plenty of oral practice before asking them to write the different kinds of nouns. Emphasize to students that a **noun** *names* a person, place, thing, or idea. Words like *he, she, it, we, you,* and *they* also may *refer to* a person, place, thing, or idea, but these are not nouns, because they do not *name*. Instead, they stand in for a noun, and are called **pronouns**. Pronouns will be introduced formally in a later lesson.

There are many words that could be either a noun or a verb (a word that shows action), depending on the context of the sentence. Write these sentences on the board and discuss this with students.

The Lord is my <u>light</u>. The Lord <u>lights</u> my way.

Another thing to consider is that some nouns may be classified more than one way, depending on how you think about them. For example, in this selection, an *army* might be categorized as persons or as a thing. Have students explain their answers, but give them much latitude. The goal is to have them begin to recognize nouns. Thinking about which of the four the noun names is a way to double-check that a word really is a noun. Nouns that name ideas can be particularly tricky. Tell students that *ideas* cannot be perceived with our senses - seeing, smelling, touching, tasting, or hearing.

Review this lesson orally all week and in the coming weeks. Look for nouns in anything you are reading. For the sake of space, and to keep the lesson length short, students are instructed to write nouns of one or two types. But repeat this lesson orally with all types of nouns. Make a game of this. Have students think of nouns that relate to a particular context and categorize them. For example, in relation to school, the students might come up with *teacher*, *schoolroom*, *book*, and *history*; in relation to sports, they might think of *coach*, *ballfield*, *basketball*, and *victory*. Repeat these activities often for mastery.

Nouns Naming Persons: Lord, foes

Nouns Naming Places: house, tent

Nouns Naming Things: light, rock

Nouns Naming Ideas: salvation, beauty

Day 2 *Rhyming Words*
Answers (will vary): meek, week, weak, leak, shriek

Day 3 *Antonyms*
Feel free to give students plenty of help with these exercises.

Answers: good, righteous, upright; allies, friends; shadow, darkness

Day 3 *Homonyms & Synonyms*
Homonym: daze

Synonyms (will vary): evil, corrupt; adversaries, foes, opponents; live, remain, reside

34

Day 4 *Past Tense & Plural*

Past Tense: advanced, fell, broke, resided, sought, kept

Plural: armies, days, beauties

℞ NATURE STUDY

Plains, Hills, Mountains, Valleys Introduce this lesson with *Home Geography* lessons:

✓ Lesson XI: Plains

✓ Lesson XII: Hills, Mountains, and Valleys

It will be easiest for students to have a picture to imitate. The one found in *Home Geography* is nice, although it may be a bit too small for students to see easily. Check history, geography, or travel books, or check the internet for other pictures to imitate.

Continue to review direction and compass orientation.

AUTUMN, WEEK 4

from THE REAL PRINCESS

One evening a fearful tempest arose, it thundered and lightened, and the rain poured down from the sky in torrents: besides, it was as dark as pitch. All at once there was heard a violent knocking at the door, and the old King, the Prince's father, went out himself to open it. ✓

It was a Princess who was standing outside the door. What with the rain and the wind, she was in a sad condition; the water trickled down from her hair, and her clothes clung to her body. She said she was a real Princess.

"Ah! we shall soon see that!" thought the old Queen-mother; however, she said not a word of what she was going to do; but went quietly into the bedroom, took all the bed-clothes off the bed, and put three little peas on the bedstead. She then laid twenty mattresses one upon another over the three peas, and put twenty feather beds over the mattresses.

~ Hans Christian Andersen

ℭ COPYBOOK & DICTATION

Our copybook selection this week is from another version of the fairy tale *How to Tell a True Princess* (sometimes called *The Princess and the Pea*) which students read in their Narration lesson last week. This is our first copybook selection in *Primer Two Autumn* with quotations. Make sure students carefully observe where the punctuation and capitalization are placed.

ℭ SPELLING, GRAMMAR, & WORD USAGE

Day 1 *Noun Review* After students have identified the possessive names in the selection on Day 1, ask them what belongs to the Prince in the selection (father).

Persons: King, father (*if students say* Prince's, *accept that as well*), Queen-mother, Princess

Things: tempest, rain, sky, door

Possessive Noun: Prince's

Day 2 *Singular & Plural Nouns*
Plural nouns from the selection: torrents, clothes, bed-clothes, peas, mattresses, beds

Make plurals: tempests, rain *or* rains, skies, winds, fathers, Princesses, mattresses, feathers, peas

Singluar/plural: The Princesses were standing outside the door.

Day 3 Synonyms, Antonyms, & Homonyms
Synonyms (will vary): loud *(in context of the model)*; genuine, actual

Antonyms (will vary): quiet, gentle; fake

Homonyms: herd; hare, heir

Day 4 Simile
Answer: dark *is compared to* pitch

ଓଃ NATURE STUDY
Rivers Introduce this lesson with *Home Geography* lessons:

   Lesson XV: How Vapor Is Changed Into Water

   Lesson XVI: Dew, Clouds, and Rain

   Lesson XXVII: How Rivers Are Made

   Lesson XXVIII: More About Rivers

   Lesson XXI: Work of Flowing Rivers

There are some fun and interesting activities in these lessons. You may wish to do them over several days. Lesson XXII is an imaginative story retelling the water cycle. We will learn more about the water cycle in *Primer Two Spring*.

AUTUMN, WEEK 5

from THE LION, THE WITCH, AND THE WARDROBE

Once there were four children whose names were Peter, Susan, Edmund, and Lucy. This story is about something that happened to them when they were sent away from London during the war because of the air-raids. They were sent to the house of an old Professor who lived in the heart of the country, ten miles from the nearest post office. He had no wife and he lived in a very large house with a housekeeper called Mrs. Macready and three servants. (Their names were Ivy, Margaret, and Betty, but they do not come into the story much.) He himself was a very old man with shaggy white hair which grew over most of his face as well as on his head, and they liked him almost at once; but on the first evening when he came out to meet them at the front door he was so odd-looking that Lucy (who was the youngest) was a little afraid of him, and Edmund (who was the next youngest) wanted to laugh and had to keep on pretending he was blowing his nose to hide it.

As soon as they had said good night to the Professor and gone upstairs on the first night, the boys came into the girls' room and they all talked it over.

"We've fallen on our feet and no mistake," said Peter. "This is going to be perfectly splendid. That old chap will let us do anything we like."

~ C. S. Lewis

☙ COPYBOOK & DICTATION

The first paragraph of this selection is very long, so the copybook exercise is divided over two days. On Day 1, copy through the first parenthetical sentence (Their names were Ivy...). Finish the paragraph on Day 2.

☙ SPELLING, GRAMMAR, & WORD USAGE
Day 1 *Noun Review*

Places: London, house, country, upstairs, room

Possessive Nouns: Peter's, Professor's, house's, man's, child's, country's

Singular/Plural: child, houses, countries, servant, men, boy

Day 2 *Common & Proper Nouns*
Discuss these examples with students before they do the written exercises:

> *The common noun* boy *can refer to any young male person. The proper noun* John *refers to a particular boy.*

> *The common noun* river *can refer to any flowing stream of water. The proper noun* Nile River *refers to a particular river.*

> *The common noun* independence *refers to the idea of freedom. The proper noun* Independence Day *refers to a particular day when that idea is celebrated.*

Give lots of oral practice in classifying nouns as common or proper in the coming weeks.

Proper (persons): Peter, Lucy, Edmund, Susan, Professor, Mrs. Macready

Proper (place): London

Common (persons): man, chap, servants

Common (places): house, country

Day 3 *Suffixes: Changing* f *to* v This lesson focuses on the

39

letter **f** at the end of a word and how it affects the addition of suffixes. The sounds of **f** and **v** are closely related. Say them aloud - your lips and tongue are in the same position for both sounds. But **f** is an *unvoiced* phonogram, while **v** is a *voiced* phonogram—it buzzes when you say it. You may introduce this idea to students, but the main thing to emphasize here is the importance of correct pronunciation to correct spelling. Have the students pronounce aloud the singular form of these words followed by the plural form to hear the distinction.

Singular nouns: wife, loaf, knife

Plural nouns: calves, lives, wolves

Singular/plural: wives, calf, life, loaves, knives, wolf; cliffs, chiefs, roofs

Day 4
Synonyms (will vary) : guy, fellow, gentleman, (grandfather, brother, son, husband, etc.); grand, magnificent, impressive

Antonyms (will vary): hated, despised, disliked; common, ordinary, unimpressive

CR NATURE STUDY
Maps Introduce this lesson with *Home Geography* lessons:

Lesson XXIV: A Map

Lesson XXV: Forms of Land and Water

Lesson XVI: More About Forms of Land and Water

A Trip to the Highlands in Lesson XVII is a nice little story to review the concepts learned in these lessons.

For the Nature Notebook activity, students may choose from several options for drawing a map. Younger students may copy a map from a storybook or from a simple and uncluttered child's atlas. Find a map that includes several of the landforms we have studied already. Older students may try their hand at drawing a map of their local area. Or they may wish to create a map of a fictional land, either from a book or from their own imaginations.

All students should include the compass rose, oriented correctly, on their maps.

AUTUMN, WEEK 6

OCTOBER'S PARTY

October gave a party;
The leaves by hundreds came —
The Chestnuts, Oaks, and Maples,
And leaves of every name.

The Sunshine spread a carpet,
And everything was grand,
Miss Weather led the dancing,
Professor Wind the band.

The Chestnuts came in yellow,
The Oaks in crimson dressed;
The lovely Misses Maple
In scarlet looked their best;

All balanced to their partners,
And gaily fluttered by;
The sight was like a rainbow

41

New fallen from the sky.

Then, in the rustic hollow,
At hide-and-seek they played,
The party closed at sundown,
And everybody stayed.

Professor Wind played louder;
They flew along the ground;
And then the party ended
In jolly "hands around."

~ George Cooper

ℭ COPYBOOK & DICTATION

The poet here is using the literary device of **personification.** Leaves and trees, which are inanimate objects, are given qualities and actions of living things. You may wish to point this out to students. Personification is formally introduced in *Primer Two Winter.*

ℭ SPELLING, GRAMMAR, & WORD USAGE

Note in the Day 2 lesson that when a plural noun or pronoun is made possessive, sometimes the thing which that noun or pronoun possesses must be made plural as well. Ask students if they notice any plural nouns that do not change from the singular in this list (the leaves all together may make a collective flight rather than individual flights; music is the same for both singular and plural). Also, the noun *children* is plural but does not end in an **s**, so the possessive is formed by adding an apostrophe plus **s.**

Day 1 *Noun Review*
Proper: October, Chestnuts, Oaks, Maples, Sunshine, Miss

Weather, Professor Wind

Common: party, leaves, carpet, band, partners, sight, rainbow, sky, hollow, sundown, ground

Day 2 *Plural Possessive Nouns*
Possessives in model: October's

Possessive Forms: in the box below leaves' flights, Oaks' dresses, children's game, bands' music, Sunshine's carpet

Day 3 *Noun Titles & Abbreviations*
Answers: Mr., Mrs., St., Prof., Rev., Dr., Capt., Gen.

Plural Title and Name: Misses Maple

Day 4 *Homonyms*
Homonyms (will vary): buy, bye; knew

Day 4 *Simile*
Similes: sight *is compared to* a rainbow

Day 4 *Rhyming Words*
Rhyming Words (will vary): cloak, soak, smoke, bloke, choke, yoke, yolk (the l is silent)

CR NATURE STUDY

Tree Leaf Identification In *Primer One Autumn*, students learned basic tree identification by observing tree leaves.

Continue to collect leaves from trees near your home or school. Try to get intact leaves. If possible, collect the seed of the tree as well. Some common seed types include cones, acorns, or helicopters. If the tree you are observing is in an area where you are not allowed to remove leaves and seeds, make very careful notes and drawings to aid you in identification. You may also make good use of technology by taking digital photos for this step.

Observe the tree. Do a quick sketch the shape of the whole tree in your nature notebook. Look at how the leaves are arranged on each stem, and make sketches. Is there only one leaf on a stem, or are there multiple leaves on the stem? If there are multiple leaves, look carefully at how the leaves are arranged on the stem. Are they directly across from each other (opposite) or do they alternate along the stem? Help students sketch and make notes as they observe.

Observe the leaf. Is it a broad leaf or a needle? What color is it? How is it shaped? Does it have a jagged, tooth-shaped edge or a smooth edge? What do the veins look like?

Bring the leaf back home and have students carefully draw it on the page provided in their *Primer* books. They should take their time and include the details you have discussed.

Using what you have collected, see if you can identify the type of tree using the links to identification keys. Students at this level should label their drawings with both the English name of the tree and the scientific (Latin) name of the tree.

Optional Enrichment Activities See the *Primer Resources Webpage* for instructions.

* Choose a tree near your house and make a sketch of it each month to observe how it changes through the year.
* Press leaves between two sheets of wax paper to

preserve them.

♦ Do leaf rubbings.

AUTUMN, WEEK 7

from THE STORY OF THE PILGRIM FATHERS

The weather was bitterly cold and the frost so keen that even their clothes were frozen stiff. And ere these Pilgrims could find a shelter from the winter blasts, trees had to be felled and hewn for the building of their houses. It was enough to make the stoutest heart quake. Yet not one among this little band of Pilgrims flinched or thought of turning back. They were made of sterner stuff than that, and they put all their trust in God.

The first winter the Pilgrim Fathers, it was said, "endured a wonderful deal of misery with infinite patience." But at length spring came, and with the coming of warmth and sunshine the sickness disappeared. The sun seemed to put new life into every one. So when in April the Mayflower, which had been in harbour all winter, sailed homeward not one of the Pilgrims sailed with her.

What was their surprise then when one morning an Indian walked boldly into the camp and spoke to them in broken English!

He told them that his name was Samoset, and that he was the Englishmen's friend. He also said he could tell them of another Indian called Squanto who could speak better English than he could. This Squanto had been stolen away from his home by a wicked captain who intended to sell him as a slave to Spain. But he had escaped to England, and later by the help of Englishmen had been brought back to his home. All his tribe however had meantime been swept away by a plague, and now only he remained.

~ This Country of Ours, H.E. Marshall

ℭ Spelling, Grammar, & Word Usage

Day 1 *The Pronoun* In this selection, the pronoun *she* is used to stand in for a ship. This is another example of personification. Sailors have traditionally referred to their ships as feminine—perhaps because they loved their ships and because they were so dependent upon them for life and sustenance. Look for additional examples of nouns which are associated with masculine or feminine pronouns.

Sentences: They felled trees and used *them* to build houses. *She* sailed, but not one of *them* sailed with her. *It* swept *them* away, and *he* alone remained.

Day 2 *Suffixes ~ Dropping a Silent e*
Answers: clothing, quaking, enduring, coming, surprising, naming, making, slaving, escaping; clothed, quaked, thought, made, endured, seemed, put, walked, swept

Day 3 *Possessive Nouns & Pronouns*
Possessive Noun: Englishmen's friend - *Englishmen* is plural

Possessive forms: their houses, our trust, his English, her sails

Day 4 *Noun Review*
Proper: Samoset, Englishmen's, Indian, Squanto, Spain, England, Englishmen

Common: weather, frost, clothes, shelter, blasts, trees, houses, heart, band, stuff, trust

Synonyms: homes, huts, dwellings; astonishment, amazement, shock

ⳗ Nature Study

Tree Leaf Identification See Week 6 Nature Study Teaching Notes.

Autumn, Week 8

Come, Ye Thankful People, Come

Come, ye thankful people, come,
Raise the song of harvest home!
All is safely gathered in,
Ere the winter storms begin;
God, our Maker, doth provide
For our wants to be supplied;
Come to God's own temple, come;
Raise the song of harvest home!

We ourselves are God's own field,
Fruit unto His praise to yield;
Wheat and tares together sown
Unto joy or sorrow grown;
First the blade and then the ear,
Then the full corn shall appear;
Lord of harvest, grant that we
Wholesome grain and pure may be.

For the Lord our God shall come,
And shall take the harvest home;
From His field shall in that day
All offenses purge away,
Give His angels charge at last
In the fire the tares to cast;
But the fruitful ears to store
In His garner evermore.

Even so, Lord quickly come,
To Thy final harvest home;
Gather Thou Thy people in,

Free from sorrow, free from sin,
There, forever purified,
In Thy presence to abide;
Come, with all Thine angels, come,
Raise the glorious harvest home!

~ Henry Alford

ᘓ Copybook & Dictation

See *A Note About Names Referring to the Trinity* in the Copybook section of Pedagogy and Practice.

ᘓ Spelling, Grammar, & Word Usage
Day 1 Compound Words with Full The rule also applies to all (all + ways → always; all + ready → already, all + together → altogether). You may wish to show students these words also.

✓ *Compound Words*: thankful, joyful, sorrowful, fruitful

Day 1 Rhyming Pairs
Endings spelled differently: purified & abide

Possible Rhymes (will vary): sown (from the selection), shown, groan, loan, phone, sewn.

Day 2 Noun Review
Proper nouns (persons, all names for God): God, Maker, Lord

Common nouns (places): home, temple, field, garner (*may also be considered a thing; can mean either a granary or a store or a supply*)

Common nouns (things): song, storms, fruit, wheat, tares,

blade, ear, corn, grain, harvest, fire

Common nouns (ideas): praise, joy, sorrow, offenses, sin, presence

Plural common noun (persons): people, person

Day 3 *Archaic* **Pronouns**
Sentence: God's thankful people are His own field

Possessive Forms: our wants, God's temple, His praise, Thy people, Your presence, its home

Day 4 Homonyms & Antonyms
Homonyms: inn, tears

Antonyms (examples): sorrow, tares (Ask students to read the line where *wheat* and *tares* appear together as antonyms.)

Ꭳꝶ NATURE STUDY
Tree Leaf Identification See Week 6 Nature Study Teaching Notes.

AUTUMN, WEEK 9
_____

from THE BURGESS ANIMAL BOOK FOR CHILDREN

Peter had been looking along that little ridge and had discovered that it ended only a short distance from him. Now as he looked at it again, he saw the flat surface of the ground at the end of the ridge rise as if being pushed up from beneath, and that little ridge became just so much longer. Peter understood perfectly. Out of sight beneath the surface Miner the Mole was at work. He was digging a tunnel, and that ridge was simply the roof to that tunnel. It was so near the surface of the ground that Miner simply pushed up the loose soil as he bored his way along, and this made the little ridge over which Peter had stumbled.

Peter watched a few minutes, then turned and scampered, lipperty-lipperty-lip, for the Green Forest. He arrived at school quite out of breath, the last one. Old Mother Nature was about to chide him for being late, but noticing his excitement, she changed her mind.

"Well, Peter," said she. "What is it now? Did you have a narrow escape on your way here?"

~ Thornton Burgess

○੪ Spelling, Grammar, & Word Usage
Day 1 Suffixes: One Syllable Base Word
Answers: digging, sinning, sunning, hopping, tracking (you only HEAR one consonant), fixing (you HEAR two consonants), rising, working, pushing, stumbling, arriving, chiding

Day 2 Noun Review
Proper nouns (persons): Peter, Miner the Mole, Old Mother Nature

Proper noun (place): Green Forest

Common nouns (places): ridge, ground, surface, tunnel, school

Singular/plural: ridges, sights, minute, pushes, roofs (the **f** is unvoiced), escape

Day 3 Past Tense
Past Tense: looked, rose, understood, dug, bored, stumbled, watched, scampered, noticed, chided, hopped, skipped

Day 4 *Onomatopoeia*

Onomatopoeia: meow or purr, buzz, hiss, roar, babble, squeal ~~gurgle~~

℥ Nature Study

Mammals Mammals for students to observe should not be too difficult to find. Subjects might include pets in your own home, friendly squirrels and chipmunks in your yard, farm animals, or animals at the zoo. Siblings and fellow students are mammals too. ✓

Begin by reviewing the characteristics of mammals. See if students can name an animal besides a mammal that also has each listed characteristic.

✓ *Mammals have a backbone.* Show students how to locate their own backbones. Explain how the backbone gives structure to the whole body. Find a picture of a human or animal skeleton and point out the backbone. Tell students that the backbone, also called the spine, is actually made up of many bones called **vertebrae** (singular **vertebra**). Animals with backbones are called **vertebrates**. Besides mammals, a few other vertebrates are fish, reptiles, and birds.

✓ *Mammals are warm-blooded.* The animal's body temperature remains constant, as opposed to a cold-blooded animal whose body temperature is determined by its environment. Birds are warm-blooded. Snakes, reptiles, insects, and fish are cold-blooded.

✓ *Mammals have lungs and breathe air.* Mammals breathe in oxygen and give off carbon dioxide. Other animals

51

with lungs include birds, amphibians, and reptiles. Fish do not have lungs, but they have gills to take in oxygen from the water.

✓ *Mammals have skin with hair on it.* Some animals, such as bears, have a lot of hair or fur; some, such as humans, have very little hair in comparison. Do birds have hair? How about fish or reptiles?

✓ *Most mammals give birth to live young.* A few mammals, like the platypus, do lay eggs instead of giving birth to live young, but this is a rare exception. Birds, fish, insects, and most reptiles lay eggs; there are a few reptiles that give birth to live young.

✓ *Mammals feed their young with milk.* All mammals have *mammary glands* which produce milk to feed their young—hence, the name *mammal.* Birds bring worms and berries to their young; insects lay their eggs where their young can find food when they hatch.

Help students think of ten mammals. Ask students to start in their own homes or yards by naming pets that might be mammals. Next ask them to name some farm animals. Then ask them to name wild animals in the meadows or woodlands (or prairie or desert) of your area. Finally, ask students to name some more exotic animals they have seen at the zoo or read about in books. If you are not sure whether a particular animal is a mammal, an internet search or a field guide should help you figure it out. There are many, many animals, but here is a short list in case you get stuck: dog, cat, horse, cow, sheep, goat, pig, lion, tiger, bear, monkey, squirrel, mouse, chipmunk, fox, beaver, rabbit, skunk, groundhog, opossum, deer, and human.

Students will choose one mammal each week to observe, discuss, and draw. Talk with students and choose which mammals they would like to study. Co-op teachers may assign different mammals to each student and ask them to give a short presentation in the next class.

If you do not have immediate access to mammals for observation, check out library books or find online resources to view and learn about specific mammals. Check the *Primer Resources Webpage* for links and resources to help with this.

The aim of these lessons is for students to simply observe a mammal and talk about it with you. Do not worry if they cannot talk about every point listed. Just ask them to keep observing through the week, and perhaps to read a little about the mammal they have chosen.

Since wild animals tend to be shy of humans and/or may be dangerous, students will probably need to use a picture to do their drawings for non-domesticated mammals. See links on the *Primer Resources Webpage*.

AUTUMN, WEEK 10

from JOHN 1

In the beginning was the Word, and the Word was with God, and the Word was God. He was in the beginning with God. All things were made through Him, and without Him nothing was made that was made. In Him was life, and the life was the light of men. And the light shines in the darkness, and the darkness did not comprehend it.

He was in the world, and the world was made through Him, and the world did not know Him. He came to His own, and His own did not receive Him. But as many as received Him, to them He gave the right to become children of God, to those who believe in His name: who were born, not of blood, nor of the will of the flesh, nor of the will of man, but of God.

And the Word became flesh and dwelt among us, and we beheld His glory, the glory as of the only begotten of the Father, full of grace and truth.

~ John 1: 1-4, 10-14, New King James Version

෯ COPYBOOK & DICTATION
See *A Note About Scripture Copybook Selections* and *A Note About Names Referring to the Trinity* in the Copybook section of Pedagogy and Practice.

෯ SPELLING, GRAMMAR, & WORD USAGE
Day 1 *Suffixes: Two Syllable Base Word*
Before you introduce the rule for adding a suffix to a two-syllable word, review the rule in for adding a suffix to a one-syllable word (see Spelling Rules & Tips in the Appendix). Discuss the need to pay close attention **accented syllables** when adding suffixes to two-syllable words. Remind them that he syllable that we pronounce most strongly is the accented syllable. Review syllable accents by writing these words on the board and letting students pronounce them with exaggerated accents:

equip (e-QUIP), commit (com-MIT), worship (WOR-ship)[1]

1 Worship *is so frequently misspelled when a suffix is added that it almost looks odd to write it properly:* worshiped, worshiping.

54

The rule says that if the accent is on the final syllable of the two-syllable word, then double to final consonant (if the word ends in one vowel and then one consonant). Work with your students on this exercise. Say each word out loud and check to see if both conditions apply, before deciding whether to double the final consonant.

Answers: beginning, begetting (present tense of *begot*, the root word of *begotten* from the selection; point out to students that *begotten* follows the rule we are learning also), forgetting, controlling, preferring, excelling, traveling (accent is on first syllable), profiting (accent is on first syllable), annoying (can see but not hear the vowel + consonant, **oy** makes the single sound /**oy**/)

Day 2 *Noun Review*

Proper nouns (persons): Word, God, Father

Common nouns (things): light, darkness, world, blood, flesh;

Common nouns (ideas): beginning *(really a verbal used as a noun, but accept it as a noun for now)*, nothing, glory, grace, truth

Singular/Plural: thing, lives, lights, darknesses, child, glories

Day 3 *Spelling Rule* ~ i *before* e
Answers: believe, receive

Day 3 *Noun & Pronoun Review*
Possessive Forms: His glory, men's lives, God's children, its Creator, gospels' truth

Day 4 *Homonyms, Synonyms, & Antonyms*

Answers (examples): gloomy *and* light; honest *and* false; start *and* end; threw, maid, knot, no, write, wright, rite

℘ Nature Study

Mammals See Week 9 Nature Study Teaching Notes. Students at this level should write both the English and Latin name of the mammals they are observing.

Autumn, Week 11

from A Christmas Carol

Such a bustle ensued that you might have thought a goose the rarest of all birds; a feathered phenomenon, to which a black swan was a matter of course—and in truth it was something very like it in that house. Mrs. Cratchit made the gravy (ready beforehand in a little saucepan) hissing hot; Master Peter mashed the potatoes with incredible vigour; Miss Belinda sweetened up the apple-sauce; Martha dusted the hot plates; Bob took Tiny Tim beside him in a tiny corner at the table; the two young Cratchits set chairs for everybody, not forgetting themselves, and mounting guard upon their posts, crammed spoons into their mouths, lest they should shriek for goose before their turn came to be helped. At last the dishes were set on, and grace was said. It was succeeded by a breathless pause, as Mrs. Cratchit, looking slowly all along the carving-knife, prepared to plunge it in the breast; but when she did, and when the long expected gush of stuffing issued forth, one murmur of delight arose all round the board, and even Tiny Tim, excited by the two young Cratchits, beat on the table with the handle of his knife, and feebly cried Hurrah!

There never was such a goose. Bob said he didn't believe there ever was such a goose cooked. Its tenderness and flavour, size and cheapness, were the themes of universal admiration. Eked out by apple-sauce and mashed potatoes, it was a sufficient dinner for the whole family; indeed, as Mrs. Cratchit said with great delight (surveying one small atom of a bone upon the dish), they hadn't ate it all at last! Yet every one had had enough, and the youngest Cratchits in particular, were steeped in sage and onion to the eyebrows! But now, the plates being changed by Miss Belinda, Mrs. Cratchit left the room alone—too nervous to bear witnesses—to take the pudding up and bring it in.

~ Charles Dickens

℞ Spelling, Grammar, & Word Usage

Point out the British spellings in this selection to students, and discuss the alternate American spellings: *vigour (vigor)*, *flavour (flavor)*. Other common examples of this spelling difference are *colour (color)*, *honour (honor)*, and *labour (labour)*. These are derived from Latin forms ending in **-or.** British spelling of these words imitated the French after the Norman Invasion, changing the **-or** to **-our.** American spelling was largely standardized by Noah Webster's 1828 Dictionary; he chose to retain the original Latin spelling.

Also, students may notice the phrase *they hadn't ate it all at last.* Dickens is quoting Mrs. Cratchit here, even though there are no quotation marks. Therefore he uses the dialect in which she would speak, with her incorrect grammar intact.

Day 1 *Possessive Pronoun* Their *& Homonyms*
Answers: their, They're, there

Day 2 *Noun Review*
Proper nouns with titles: Mrs. Cratchit, Master Peter, Miss Belinda, Tiny Tim

Common noun (ending in -o): potato, potatoes

Common nouns (things): chairs, posts, spoons, dishes

Singular/plural: plate, knives, gushes, geese, bones, Cratchit

Day 3 *Noun & Pronoun Review*
Noun/pronoun substitution: The feast (goose) was a sufficient dinner for them.; gravy's hiss, goose's flavour, its tenderness, Mrs. Cratchit's delight; The Cratchits' feast is approaching! The young Cratchits beat on the table.

✓ **Day 4 *Onomatopoeia***
Onomatopoeia: bustle, hissing, shriek, gush

Day 4 *Homonyms, Synonyms, & Antonyms*
Answers: small, huge, joy, disgust, fourth

ℭ Nature Study
Mammals See Week 9 Nature Study Teaching Notes.

Autumn, Week 12 _____

from Once in Royal David's City

> Once in royal David's city
> Stood a lowly cattle shed,
> Where a mother laid her baby
> In a manger for his bed:
> Mary was that mother mild,
> Jesus Christ her little child.
>
> He came down to earth from Heaven,
> Who is God and Lord of all,
> And his shelter was a stable,
> And his cradle was a stall;

With the poor, and mean, and lowly,
Lived on earth our Savior holy.

And our eyes at last shall see him,
Through his own redeeming love,
For that child so dear and gentle
Is our Lord in Heav'n above,
And He leads His children on
To the place where He is gone.

Not in that poor lowly stable,
With the oxen standing by,
We shall see him; but in Heaven,
Set at God's right hand on high;
Where like stars his children crowned
All in white shall wait around.

~ Cecil Frances Alexander

ℂℜ COPYBOOK & DICTATION
See *A Note About Names Referring to the Trinity* in the Copybook section of Pedagogy and Practice.

ℂℜ SPELLING, GRAMMAR, & WORD USAGE
Day 1 *Rhyming Pairs*
Endings spelled the same: shed - bed, mild - child, all - stall, love - above

Endings spelled differently: lowly - holy, on - gone, by - high, crowned - around

Words that rhyme with dear: fear, hear, steer, pier, sincere

Day 2 *Noun Review*
Proper nouns (persons): David, Mary, Jesus Christ, God, Lord, Savior

Common nouns (persons): mother, baby, child, children; (*Note: poor, mean,* and lowly *are all substantive adjectives used as nouns naming persons. Poor = poor men; mean = mean men; lowly = lowly men. If students give any of these as common nouns, you may explain this, but otherwise, this concept will be covered in a later book.*)

Common nouns (places): city, shed, manger, earth, stall, place, (*God's right*) hand, high;

Plural Forms: oxen, cattle

✓ *Possessive Forms:* David's city, God's right hand, stars' brightness

Day 3 *Possessive Pronouns* Your & Whose & *Homonyms*
Answers: Who's this baby whose mother laid Him in a manger? Jesus, you're at the right hand of your Father.

Day 4 *Homonyms, Synonyms, & Antonyms*
Answers: humble; common, lowly; dwelling, home; rough, violent; I, aye; wear

Day 4 *Simile*
Simile: his children *are compared to* stars

CⱭ NATURE STUDY
Mammals See Week 9 Nature Study Teaching Notes.

PRIMER TWO WINTER TEACHING HELPS & NOTES

WHEN MOTHER READS ALOUD

When Mother reads aloud, the past
Seems real as every day;
I hear the tramp of armies vast,
I see the spears and lances cast,
I join the thrilling fray;
Brave knights and ladies fair and proud
I meet when Mother reads aloud.

When Mother reads aloud, far lands
Seem very near and true;
I cross the deserts' gleaming sands,
Or hunt the jungle's prowling bands,
Or sail the ocean blue.
Far heights, whose peaks the cold mists shroud,
I scale, when Mother reads aloud.

✓

When Mother reads aloud, I long
For noble deeds to do —
To help the right, redress the wrong;
It seems so easy to be strong,
So simple to be true.
Oh, thick and fast the visions crowd
My eyes, when Mother reads aloud.

~ Author Unknown

℘ SPELLING, GRAMMAR, AND WORD USAGE

Remember that it is perfectly fine to help Primer students and prompt them with answers if they struggle.

✓ Nouns were introduced in *Primer Two Autumn*, Week 3. Refer to the Teaching Notes from that week as needed.

Day 1 *Rhyming Words*

Endings spelled the same: past - vast - cast, day-fray, proud

62

- aloud; lands - sands - bands, true - blue, shroud - aloud, long - wrong - strong

Endings spelled differently: do - true, crowd - aloud

Words that rhyme with spear: dear, shear, hear, here, mere, peer, pier

Day 2 *Noun Review*
Persons: Mother - proper; armies, knights, ladies - common ✓

Places: lands, desert, sands, jungle, ocean, heights, peaks - common

Things/ideas: past, day, tramp, spears, lances, fray, bands, mists, deeds, right, wrong, visions, eyes

Note: right *and* wrong *are* **substantive adjectives** *used as nouns. Right = right things and wrong = wrong things. If students give any these as nouns naming things or ideas, you may explain this. This concept will be covered in a later book.)*

Singular/plural: days, army, lance, knight, lady, eyes ✓

Day 3 *Possessive Nouns & Pronouns*
Possessive forms: armies' tramps, knight's lance; heights' peaks, ocean's waves

Possessives in the model: deserts' (gleaming) sands, jungle's (prowling) bands, my eyes

Day 4 *Homonyms, Synonyms, & Antonyms*
Feel free to give students plenty of help with these exercises.

Homonyms: passed; reel

63

Synonyms & Antonyms (will vary): immense; craven or cowardly; climb; complicated

NATURE STUDY[1]

> *"The heavens declare the glory*
> *of God . . ." ~ Psalm 19:1*

Review the instructions for Nature Study in the Pedagogy & Practice section of the Introduction.

The phases of the moon and several of the most easily recognized constellations were introduced in Primer One, and are reviewed here because every student should learn them well. Primer Two students are given a few additional challenges along with these. See links on the *Primer Resources Webpage* for additional constellations to study.

✓

The Night Sky Before you read this introduction to students, write the bolded words on the board.

> **Astronomy**, the study of the heavens, is said to be the most ancient of the sciences. References to the heavens — the sun, the moon, and the stars — are plentiful in literature, legends, folklore, and especially in Scripture. Psalm 19:1 tells us, "The heavens declare the glory of God..." These nature study lessons are designed to introduce you the glories of the night sky, as you begin to make your own observations about them.
>
> The moon's appearance changes every night,

✓

1 All information about constellations in the Primer series is from the perspective of North America. If you live in a different location, you will need to adjust. See the Primer Resources Webpage for online resources.

going from a tiny crescent sliver to a big round circle (**Full Moon**), then back to a sliver before it disappears for a night or two (**New Moon**). The changes in the shape of the moon through the 28 day **lunar cycle** are called **phases**. Check the *Primer Resources Webpage* for links to websites where the monthly **lunar phases** are illustrated.

We say that the moon is **waxing** as it goes from a **New Moon** to a **Full Moon**, and we say it is **waning** as it moves from a **Full Moon** back to a **New Moon**. In both of these periods, we see a **crescent** shape and a **gibbous** shape. The word gibbous comes from Latin word *gibbus*, meaning *hump*.

You can tell whether the moon is waxing or waning by looking at the **horns** or points of the crescent. When the horns point to the left, the moon is **waxing**. When the horns point to the right, the moon is **waning**.

Did you know that each month's moon has a name? You have probably heard of the **Harvest Moon**, which is in September or October. How do you suppose it got its name? (*It occurs during the time when farmers are harvesting their crops. Farmers are able to work in their fields by the light of the moon far into the night for several days around the time of the full moon.*)

Native Americans had names for each moon of the year. The *Farmer's Almanac* lists some of these (see *Primer Resources Webpage* for link).

Students are instructed to keep a calendar of the phases of the moon for one month. The winter months are a good time to do this with earlier nightfall and moonrise. Help students make a calendar in their nature notebooks on two facing pages with blanks large enough to draw and label the phases of the moon through the month.

WINTER, WEEK 2

from PRINCE CASPIAN

It was long and steep, but when they came out on the roof of the tower and Caspian had got his breath, he felt that it had been well worth it. On his left was the gleam of the Great River, and everything was so quiet that he could hear the sound of the waterfall at Beaversdam, a mile away. There was no difficulty in picking out the two stars they had come to see. They hung rather low in the southern sky, almost as bright as two little moons and very close together.

"Are they going to have a collision?" he asked in an awestruck voice.

"Nay, dear Prince," said the Doctor (and he too spoke in a whisper). "The great lords of the upper sky know the steps of their dance too well for that. Look well upon them. Their meeting is fortunate and means some great good for the sad realm of Narnia. Tarva, the Lord of Victory, salutes Alambil, the Lady of Peace. They are just coming to their nearest."

"It's a pity that tree gets in the way," said Caspian. "We'd really see better from the West Tower, though it is not so high."

Doctor Cornelius said nothing for about two minutes, but stood still with his eyes fixed on Tarva and Alambil. Then he drew a deep breath and turned to Caspian.

"There," he said. "You have seen what no man now alive has seen, nor will see again."

C.S. Lewis

❧ COPYBOOK & DICTATION

Note that the first word of each paragraph of prose is indented. In typeset, you will sometimes see paragraphs that are not indented when they are separated by a line, as in this book. Show this to students, but always have them indent when they are writing by hand.

❧ SPELLING, GRAMMAR, AND WORD USAGE

Recognizing the verb in a sentence is vital to understanding how sentences work, Yet this can be somewhat tricky, since verbs are very commonly used as or transformed into other parts of speech. In *Primer Two*, the aim is to build familiarity with the concept of a verb; mastery will come much later.

The easiest type of **verb** for students to recognize is one that *expresses action*. Give students plenty of oral practice in recognizing or thinking of words that may be used as vowels. Ask students to think of all the actions they perform each morning: *wake, arise, brush, pray, read, etc.*

Remind them that there are many words that could be either a verb or a noun, depending on the context of the sentence. Write the sentences below (from *Primer Two Autumn*, Week 3) on the board once more and discuss the different meanings of the word *light* in each:

The Lord is my light. The Lord lights my way.

On Day 2, the idea of verbs expressing *being* or *state* is introduced. This is necessary for a complete understanding of verbs, but please do not worry about having students understand the fine distinctions between being and state.

Verb phrases are also taught on Day 2. It is not necessary to ask students to understand the technical terms *helping verb* or *auxiliary verb* at this point.

Review this lesson orally all this week and in the coming weeks, focusing on verbs that express action. Look for verbs in anything you are reading. Discuss the actions you perform as you go through your day, and think of the verbs which express those actions. Make a game of it. Have students think of verbs that relate to a particular context. For example, in relation to school, the students might come up with *read, write, study*; in relation to sports, they might think of *run, jump, throw*, etc. Repeat these activities often for mastery.

Day 1 *Verbs Expressing Action*
Verbs to complete sentences (may vary): came, spoke, knew, drew, turned

Verbs that can be either nouns or verbs: sound, whisper, salutes. There may be others, but these are the most obvious. (*Note: students may correctly identify* left *as a word that can either be used as a noun or a verb, but it is technically a substantive adjective. See Week 1, Day 2.*)

Day 2 *Verbs Expressing Being or State*
Verbs: is, seems, was; have seen, has seen, will see

Day 3 *Spelling Rule: Silent e with Soft c or g*
Answers: dancing (the **i** after the **c** keeps the **c** soft, so the **e** can be dropped), dancer (the **e** in the **-er** ending keeps the **c** soft, so the silent **e** can be dropped), danced (the **e** in the **-ed** ending keeps the c soft, so the silent **e** can be dropped),

peaceful (silent **e** is kept so the **c** remains soft), peaceable (silent e is kept so the **c** remains soft), courageous (silent **e** is kept so the **g** remains soft), changing (the **i** in the **-ing** ending keeps the **g** soft, so the silent e can be dropped), changed (the **e** in the **-ed** ending keeps the **g** soft, so the silent **e** can be dropped), changeable (silent **e** is kept so the **g** remains soft), forcing (the **i** in the **-ing** ending keeps the **g** soft, so the silent **e** can be dropped), forced (the **e** in the **-ed** ending keeps the **g** soft, so the silent **e** can be dropped), forceful (silent **e** is kept so the **c** remains soft)

Day 4 Personification

Personification: frost *painted;* wind *whispered; wise* owl; (You might also ask students to point out the simile in the selection: *as bright as two little moons.*)

○℞ NATURE STUDY

The Constellations Before you read this introduction to students, write the bolded words on the board.

When you look up at the sky on a clear night, what do you see? Hundreds, thousands, even millions of stars twinkling in inky darkness. Truly, "the heavens declare the glory of God." (Psalm 19)

Think about this: the stars you see in the night sky are the same stars that shone over Nazareth when Jesus was a boy. They are the same stars that delighted and intrigued the ancient Greeks, and that helped guide Columbus and his men to America.

From the beginning of recorded history, men have noticed groupings of stars that seemed to make pictures in the sky. These star groupings are called **constellations**, and most of them are still known by the names that the ancient Greeks gave to them.

If you live away from the lights of a city or town, on a clear night you can see The **Milky Way**, a hazy ribbon that looks almost like dust stretching across the sky. What you are seeing is one of the spiral arms of our own galaxy of stars. The ancient Greeks said that the Milky Way was the pathway to the throne room of the gods on Mount Olympus.

It is fun to learn the name of constellations and to be able to recognize them in the night sky. Over the next few weeks, we will learn some of the most familiar.

Check the *Primer Resources Webpage* for a free interactive sky map where you can put in the name of the city nearest you. For information on the compass rose, see Autumn Week 1 *Home Geography* Lessons.

Optional Enrichment Read stories that the ancient Greeks made up to explain the the constellations. See the *Primer Resources Webpage*.

WINTER, WEEK 3

from JOB 38

"Where were you when I laid the foundations of the earth?
    Tell Me, if you have understanding.
    Who determined its measurements?
    Surely you know!
    Or who stretched the line upon it?
    To what were its foundations fastened?
    Or who laid its cornerstone,
    When the morning stars sang together,
    And all the sons of God shouted for joy?"

"Can you bind the cluster of the Pleiades,
    Or loose the belt of Orion?
    Can you bring out Mazzarothin its season?
    Or can you guide the Great Bear with its cubs?
    Do you know the ordinances of the heavens?
    Can you set their dominion over the earth?"

~Job 38: 4-7, 31-33, New King James Version

⊘ COPYBOOK & DICTATION
See *A Note About Scripture Copybook Selections* and *A Note About Names Referring to the Trinity* in the Copybook section of Pedagogy and Practice.

⊘ SPELLING, GRAMMAR, AND WORD USAGE
One way to help students think about simple past, present, and future tense is by using the words *yesterday, today,* and *tomorrow.* Choose any verb, and have students put it in a sentence for each tense: *Yesterday I threw the ball. Today I*

throw the ball. Tomorrow I shall throw the ball. Students have already been working with past tense verbs in the spelling exercises. Continue practicing this orally often.

Day 1 *Verb Tense*
Sentences: The morning stars sang together. The morning stars will sing together. The Pleiades were in the night sky. The Pleiades will be in the night sky.

Day 2 *Noun Review*
Proper nouns naming constellations: Pleiades, Orion, Mazzarothin, Great Bear

Ideas: foundations, understanding, measurements, line, cornerstone, season, ordinances, dominion

Places or things: earth, stars, cluster, belt, cubs, heavens;

Possessive forms: foundations of earth, its cornerstone, Orion's belt, heavens' ordinances

Day 3 *Verb Review*
Sentences: I guided the Great Bear with its cubs. I will guide the Great Bear with its cubs. Earth's cornerstones were fastened. Earth's cornerstones will be fastened.

Day 4 ~ *Homonyms, Synonyms, & Antonyms*
Homonyms: layed, lade; it's

Synonyms & antonyms (will vary): decrees, statutes; whispered; authority, rule; loosed, detached, released

ᐸᑌ NATURE STUDY
Ursa Major and the Big Dipper Before you read this

introduction to students, write the bolded words on the board.

> The **Big Dipper** is one of the most familiar star groupings, although it is not technically a constellation in its own right but is part of a larger constellation called **Ursa Major** (the Big Bear). Star groupings like this within a constellation are called **asterisms**. Because many of the stars in Ursa Major are faint, it is hard to see the entire constellation. But the Big Dipper, the asterism made by the seven brightest stars in Ursa Major, is easily seen. See the *Primer Resources Webpage* for a link to help you identify the Big Dipper.

Winter, Week 4

from Pinnochio

How it happened that Mastro Cherry, carpenter, found a piece of wood that wept and laughed like a child.

Centuries ago there lived—

"A king!" my little readers will say immediately.

No, children, you are mistaken. Once upon a time there was a piece of wood. It was not an expensive piece of wood. Far from it. Just a common block of firewood, one of those thick, solid logs that are put on the fire in winter to make cold rooms cozy and warm.

I do not know how this really happened, yet the fact remains that one fine day this piece of wood found itself in the shop of an old carpenter. His real name was Mastro Antonio, but everyone called him Mastro Cherry, for the tip of his nose was so round and red and shiny that it looked like a ripe cherry.

73

As soon as he saw that piece of wood, Mastro Cherry was filled with joy. Rubbing his hands together happily, he mumbled half to himself:

"This has come in the nick of time. I shall use it to make the leg of a table."

~ Carlo Collodi

☙ SPELLING, GRAMMAR, AND WORD USAGE

Day 1 *Singular & Plural Verbs*

You may wish to point out to students that singular verbs often have an -s added at the end. This is just the opposite of nouns. Examples: *He sings. They sing.* But this is not a hard and fast rule. What if the subject is *I*? *I sing.* That is why we tell students they must look at the subject in order to determine whether a particular verb is singular or plural.

Sentences: The carpenters found pieces of wood. A (The) log is put on the fire. Pieces of wood were found in the shops. We shall use them to make the legs of tables.

Day 2 *Suffixes: Two Syllable Base Words*

Review the rule for adding a suffix which begins with a vowel to a two-syllable word (Autumn Week 10, and also Spelling Rules & Tips in the Appendix).

Answers: happened, commonly (suffix does not begin with a vowel), winterize (accent is on the first syllable), permitting, disobeyed (can see but not hear the vowel + consonant, **ey** makes the single sound /**ay**/), worshiper (accent is on first syllable), renewal (can see but not hear the vowel + consonant, **ew** makes the single sound /ū/), commitment (suffix does not begin with a vowel), rebellion

Day 3 *Verb Review*
Present: The old carpenter is filled with joy.

Future: The old carpenter will be filled with joy.

Singular/Plural: They rub their hands together happily.

Day 3 *Homonyms, Synonyms, & Antonyms*
Homonyms: would

Synonyms & antonyms (will vary): woodworker, despair

Day 4 *Spelling Rule:* i *before* e
Answer: piece

ᛒ NATURE STUDY
The Little Dipper and Polaris Before you read this introduction to students, find the link to a picture of the Little Dipper on the *Primer Resources Webpage*. Write the bolded words on the board.

> Notice how the *bowl* of the **Big Dipper** points in a staight line toward the **North Star,** or **Polaris**. Polaris is the brightest star in the **Little Dipper,** the familiar asterism in the constellation of **Ursa Minor** (the Little Bear).
>
> Polaris is a very important star, because it is a *fixed* star, always directly above the horizon at due north. The other stars appear to rotate around it. Because of this, Polaris can always be used for finding direction at night.

Teach this lesson with oral exercises from *Home Geography:*

Lesson III: How the Stars Show Direction

WINTER, WEEK 5

STOPPING BY WOODS

Whose woods these are I think I know.
His house is in the village though;
He will not see me stopping here
To watch his woods fill up with snow.

My little horse must think it queer
To stop without a farmhouse near
Between the woods and frozen lake
The darkest evening of the year.

He gives his harness bells a shake
To ask if there is some mistake.
The only other sound's the sweep
Of easy wind and downy flake.

The woods are lovely, dark and deep.
But I have promises to keep,
And miles to go before I sleep,
And miles to go before I sleep.

~ Robert Frost

Ꮖ SPELLING, GRAMMAR, AND WORD USAGE

Technically, the **subject** of a sentence is the subject noun and all its modifiers; the **predicate** of a sentence is the verb and all its modifiers. The subject noun is sometimes called the **simple subject**, and the verb or verb phrase telling what the subject is or does is called the **simple predicate**. Students will learn these distinctions later. For now, just mark the subject noun or pronoun and the predicate verb or verb phrase.

Day 1 *Subjects & Predicates*
Subjects: Snow, horse, woods, I

Predicate Verbs: fills, gives, are, have

Day 2 *Rhyming Words*
Rhyming Words: know - though - snow, here - near - queer - year; lake - shake - mistake - flake; sweep - deep - keep - sleep - sleep

Day 3 *Subjects & Predicates*
Answers: He will not see me here. He does not see me here. He did not see me here. He stops without a farmhouse near. They stop without a farmhouse near. I have miles to go. We have miles to go.

Day 3 *Personification & Onomatopoeia*
Personfication: the horse is given human attributes of thinking and asking

Onomatopoeia: sweep

Day 4 *Contractions*
Answers: I've, can't, mustn't, it's, won't, sound's = sound + is

ᘓ Nature Study
Cassiopeia Before you read this introduction to students, write the bolded words on the board.

> Cassiopeia is in the north sky. Find the **Big Dipper**, then find **Polaris**. Look on the other side of Polaris from the Big Dipper. You should see

five bright stars that make a sort of sideways W in the sky. That is **Cassiopeia.**

WINTER, WEEK 6

A LACONIC ANSWER

Many miles beyond Rome there was a famous country which we call Greece. The people of Greece were not united like the Romans; but instead there were several states, each of which had its own rulers. Some of the people in the southern part of the country were called Spartans, and they were noted for their simple habits and their bravery. The name of their land was Laconia, and so they were sometimes called Lacons.

One of the strange rules which the Spartans had, was that they should speak briefly, and never use more words than were needed. And so a short answer is often spoken of as being *laconic*; that is, as being such an answer as a Lacon would be likely to give.

There was in the northern part of Greece a land called Macedon; and this land was at one time ruled over by a war-like king named Philip. Philip of Macedon wanted to become the master of all Greece. So he raised a great army, and made war upon the other states, until nearly all of them were forced to call him their king. Then he sent a letter to the Spartans in Laconia, and said, "If I go down into your country, I will level your great city to the ground."

In a few days, an answer was brought back to him. When he opened the letter, he found only one word written there.

That word was "IF."

It was as much as to say, "We are not afraid of you so long as the little word 'if' stands in your way."

~ James Baldwin

∞ COPYBOOK & DICTATION

The first paragraph of the selection gives the context for the story; it is not included in the week's copybook exercises.

∞ SPELLING, GRAMMAR, AND WORD USAGE

Day 1 *Correct Use of Words ~ Shall and Will*

Answers: I shall level your great city to the ground. I will level your great city to the ground. We shall not fear Philip of Macedon. We will not fear Philip of Macedon.

Day 2 *Suffixes: Base Word Ending in Silent Final -e*

Answers: mileage (silent final **e** needed to keep vowel long), uniting, ruler, bravery (suffix does not begin with a vowel), strangely (suffix does not begin with a vowel), given, raising, stating, statement (suffix does not begin with a vowel), writer, acreage (silent final **e** needed so that every syllable has a vowel), forceable (silent final **e** needed to keep **c** soft)

Day 3 *Subjects & Predicates*

Sentences: Philip raised a great army. Philip will raise a great army. Laconic answers are brief answers.

Day 4 *~ Derviatives*

Answers: Laconia, Lacons, laconic

Discuss why the first two are capitalized (proper nouns) and the third is not (common noun).

Day 4 *~ Homonyms, Synonyms, & Antonyms*

Homonyms: grease, raze

Synonyms & Antonyms (will vary): laconic, short, concise;

lengthy, long; ruler, king, lord

☙ NATURE STUDY

Orion and the Pleiades Before you read this introduction to students, write the bolded words on the board.

> Some of the brightest stars in the night sky are contained in the constellation **Orion** (also known as The Hunter). Look for Orion high in the sky in the winter months, although you can also see him in the spring and fall months as well. Look at the link to the constellations on the *Primer Resources Webpage*. You can see the shape of a man, with a sword and a belt. In fact, the three bright stars in **Orion's Belt** will help you to find this constellation. In the winter, the **Milky Way** passes right over Orion's head.
>
> Next to Orion is **Taurus**, The Bull. The seven bright stars in a V-shape, forming the head of the bull, are an asterism called **The Pleiades**.

WINTER, WEEK 7

OUR GOD, OUR HELP IN AGES PAST

Our God, our help in ages past,
Our hope for years to come,
Our shelter from the stormy blast,
And our eternal home.

Under the shadow of Thy throne
Thy saints have dwelt secure;
Sufficient is Thine arm alone,

And our defense is sure.

Before the hills in order stood,
Or earth received her frame,
From everlasting Thou art God,
To endless years the same.

A thousand ages in thy sight
Are like an evening gone;
Short as the watch that ends the night
Before the rising sun.

Time, like an ever-rolling stream,
Bears all its sons away;
They fly forgotten, as a dream
Dies at the opening day.

Our God, our help in ages past,
Our hope for years to come,
Be Thou our guard while troubles last,
And our eternal home.

~ Isaac Watts

℞ COPYBOOK & DICTATION

See *A Note About Names Referring to the Trinity* in the Copybook section of Pedagogy and Practice.

Students were introduced to archaic pronouns in *Primer Two Autumn* Week 8. This hymn has several archaic pronouns that are not in common use today: *thou, thy,* and *thine*. The word *archaic* means "from an earlier period of time". These pronouns are often used in hymns and prayers, because they were in common usage when the King James version of the Bible was written. Today, instead of *thou* and *ye* we say *you*; instead of *thy* and *thine* we say *your*. The verb *art* is the archaic word for *are*.

81

CR SPELLING, GRAMMAR, AND WORD USAGE

Day 1 Verb Tense: Past, Present, & Future

Brainstorm with students for time expressions that they may use in their sentences. Here are a few to get you started.

Past time expressions: yesterday, last week, recently, an hour ago, once upon a time, many years ago

Present time expressions: today, at this moment, now, right now, as we speak, these days

Future time expressions: tomorrow, next week, next year, in the future, someday, soon, later

Day 2 *Rhyming Words*

Rhyming words spelled the same: past - blast; come - home (slant rhyme); throne - alone; secure - sure; frame - same; sight - night; stream - dream; away - day; past - last

Rhyming words spelled differently: stood - God (slant rhyme); gone - sun (slant rhyme)

Rhyming words (will vary): bears - shares, hairs, prayers, tears, squares

Day 3 *Subjects & Predicates*

Sentences: <u>God</u> <u>is</u> our shelter and our eternal home. God was our shelter and our eternal home. God will be our shelter and our eternal home. The night <u>watch</u> <u>is</u> short. The night watches are short.

Day 4 *Onomatopoeia & Simile:*

Onomatopoeia: blast

Simile (most obvious): time *is compared to* stream; *(more subtle)* sons flying away *and* forgotten *are compared to a dream upon waking. Students may suggest* a thousand ages *being compared to* an evening. *This is a comparison, but not technically a simile, since* ages *and* evening *are related; they are both measurements of time.*

☪ NATURE STUDY

Birds Students should learn to identify the most common birds found in your area. Begin in the backyard—installing a birdfeeder is an easy and inexpensive investment that pays huge dividends in both education and enjoyment for your whole family. Planting certain types of flowers and bushes will also attract birds.

Explain and discuss the characteristics of birds. See if students can name an animal classification other than birds which also has any of the listed characteristics.

✓ *Birds have a backbone.* Show students their own backbone and ask if they remember its purpose (*to give structure to the whole body*). Find a picture of a bird skeleton and point out the backbone. Remind them of the technical term for an animal with a backbone: **vertebrate.** Besides birds, a few other animals which have backbones are mammals, fish, and reptiles. Point out to students that birds generally have very lightweight bones, and many bird bones are hollow. Ask students why this is so (*to make it easier for a bird to fly*).

✓ *Birds are warm-blooded.* The birds's body temperature remains constant, as opposed to a cold-blooded animal whose body temperature is determined by its environment. Mammals are also warm-blooded. Snakes, reptiles, insects, and fish are cold-blooded.

✓ *Birds have lungs and breathe air.* Many animals breathe in oxygen and give off carbon dioxide. Other animals with lungs include mammals, amphibians, and reptiles. Fish do not have lungs, but they have gills to take in oxygen from the water.

✓ *Birds have skin covered with feathers.* The feathers provide protection against cold and water. Do mammals have feathers? How about fish or reptiles?

✓ *Birds have wings.* All birds have wings and most birds use them to fly. There are a few flightless birds, however. Does any other type of animal have wings? (*Bats are mammals with wings. Insects also have wings.*)

✓ *Birds lay eggs instead of giving birth to live young.* The mother bird usually sits on the eggs to keep them warm until they hatch. Fish, insects, and most reptiles also lay eggs; although there are a few reptiles that give birth to live young. Mammals give birth to live young.

Help students think of ten types of birds. If they have trouble with this, an internet search or a field guide should help. There are many different types of birds, but not all of them are found in every geographic location. Here is a short list of common birds in case you get stuck: *cardinal, sparrow, bluebird, blackbird, woodpecker, owl, duck, wren, robin, hummingbird, seagull, starling, goldfinch, swallow, chicken, penguin, ostrich.*

Olive Thorne Miller's *Children's Book of Birds* (originally published in 1899 as *The First Book of Birds*) is a good book to read with your students over the next few weeks as you study birds. It is available as a free PDF download or a Kindle download at Gutenberg Project. The *Primer Resources Webpage* has a link to this.

Each week, choose a bird for students to observe, discuss, and draw in Weeks 8-12. Co-op teachers may assign different birds to individual students each week, and ask students to present their observations in the next class.

Try to choose birds that come to your bird feeder if possible. If you do not have immediate access to the bird you wish to study, check out books from the library or find online resources to view and learn about it. Check the *Primer Resources Webpage* for links and resources to help with this.

In addition to sketching the bird, *Primer Two* students are instructed to sketch the bird's beak. You may need to look this up in a field guide or on a bird identification website. Also, read Chapter XXII in *The Children's Book of Birds* about the beaks and tongues of birds. Discuss with students why the bird's beak is shaped as it is, given the needs of the bird's diet and habits.

The goal of these lessons is for students to simply observe a bird and talk about it with you. Do not worry if they cannot talk about every point. Just ask students to keep observing through the week, and perhaps to read a little about the bird they have chosen. Since wild animals tend to be shy of humans, students will probably need a picture to do their drawing. Use the *Primer Resources Webpage* to help you find pictures which students can copy.

Optional Enrichment Activities (see the *Primer Resources Webpage* for help with these activities):

 • Keep a log of birds that come to your birdfeeder.

 • Study the different types of feathers birds have.

 • Learn to recognize the songs of the birds at your birdfeeder.

 • Learn about what type of nests different birds build.

WINTER, WEEK 8

from THE CHILDREN'S BOOK OF BIRDS

Each bird mother has her own way of making the nest, but there is one thing almost all of them try to do, and that is to hide it.

They cannot put their little homes out in plain sight, as we do our houses, because so many creatures want to rob them. Squirrels and snakes and rats, and some big birds, and cats and many others, like to eat eggs and young birds.

So most birds try, first of all, to find good hiding-places. Some tiny warblers go to the tops of the tallest trees, and hide the nest among the leaves. Orioles hang the swinging cradle at the end of a branch, where cats and snakes and naughty boys cannot come. Song sparrows tuck the little home in a tuft of weeds, on the ground, and bobolinks hide it in the deep grass.

After a safe place is found, they have to get something to build of. They hunt all about and gather small twigs, or grass stems, or fine rootlets, and pull narrow strips of bark off the grapevines and the birch-trees, or they pick up strings and horsehairs, and many other things. Robins and swallows use mud.

~ Olive Thorne Miller

ℭ Spelling, Grammar, and Word Usage

Day 1 Conjunctions

Conjunctions: but (join groups of words), or (used 3 times, join groups of words), and (joins words)

Day 2 Noun Review

Name birds: warblers, sparrows, bobolinks, robins, swallows

Name mammals: squirrels, rats, cats

Name places: homes, tops, end, hiding-places, *also (in context)* ground, weeds, grass, tree, branch, leaves

Day 3 Subjects & Predicates

Answers: The <u>warbler</u> <u>builds</u> her nest in a tree. The warbler built her nest in a tree. The warbler will build her nest in a tree. Mother <u>birds</u> <u>hide</u> their nests. A mother bird hides her nest. <u>Sparrows</u> <u>tuck</u> their nests in a tuft of weeds. The sparrow tucks her (its) nest in a tuft of weeds. Safe <u>places</u> <u>are found</u>. A safe place is found.

Day 4 ~ Homonyms, Synonyms, & Antonyms

Homonyms: site, plane

Synonyms & antonyms (will vary): steal; unruly, mischevious; few; wide, broad

ℭ Nature Study

Birds See Winter Week 7 Nature Study Teaching Notes.

THE WIND

I saw you toss the kites on high
And blow the birds about the sky;
And all around I heard you pass,
Like ladies' skirts across the grass~
O wind, a-blowing all day long,
O wind, that sings so loud a song!

I saw the different things you did,
But always you yourself you hid.
I felt you push, I heard you call,
I could not see yourself at all~
O wind, a-blowing all day long,
O wind, that sings so loud a song!

O you that are so strong and cold,
O blower, are you young or old?
Are you a beast of field and tree,
Or just a stronger child than me?
O wind, a-blowing all day long,
O wind, that sings so loud a song!

~ Robert Louis Stevenson

ℭ SPELLING, GRAMMAR, AND WORD USAGE

Day 1 *Pronouns & Personification*

Personification: I toss the kites on high. I blow the birds about the sky.

Simile: the wind *is compared to* ladies' skirts.

Day 2 *Rhyming Words*

Rhyming words spelled the same: pass - grass, long - song, did - hid, call - all, cold - old

Rhyming words spelled differently: high - sky, tree - me; blowing - growing

Rhyming words (will vary): stowing, going, sewing

Day 3 *Subjects & Predicates*
Sentences: <u>You</u> <u>sing</u> so loud a song! You sang so loud a song! You will sing so loud a song! A (The) lady's skirt rustles across the grass.

Day 4 ~ *Noun & Pronoun Review*
Sentence: The poet (The boy, Robert) felt it push and call.

Possessive forms: ladies' skirts, tails of kites, wind's push, titles of poems, sparrows' homes, mischief of boys

CR NATURE STUDY
Birds See Winter Week 7 Nature Study Teaching Notes.

WINTER, WEEK 10

from HEIDI

"Why do the mountains have no names, grandfather?" asked Heidi.

"They all have names, and if you tell me their shape I can name them for you."

Heidi described several and the old man could name them all. The child told him now about all the happenings of the day, and especially about the wonderful fire. She asked how it came about.

"The sun does it," he exclaimed. "Saying good-night to the mountains, he throws his most beautiful rays to them, that they may not forget him till the morning."

Heidi was so much pleased with this explanation, that she could hardly wait to see the sun's good-night greetings repeated. It was time now to go to bed, and Heidi slept soundly all night. She dreamt that the little Snowhopper was bounding happily about on the glowing mountains with many glistening roses blooming round her.

~ Johanna Spyri

ℭℛ Spelling, Grammar, and Word Usage

Day 1 *Word Order ~ Questions*

Questions: Do the mountains have names? Are you a beast of field or tree? The mountains do have names. You are a beast of field or tree. He could name them for her. Snowhopper was bounding happily about. Could he name them for her? Was Snowhopper bounding happily about?

Day 2 *Suffixes: y changing to i*

Answers: happiness, saying, skies, fancier, dutiful, leaves, fired, soundly, timing, valleys, birches, happening

Day 3 *Subjects & Predicates*

Answers (time expressions will vary): Heidi slept soundly last night. Heidi will sleep soundly next week. Are the sun's greetings repeated? Is the sun's greeting repeated?

Day 4 ~ *Homonyms, Synonyms, & Antonyms*

Homonyms: knight, weight

Synonyms & antonyms (will vary): astonishing; ugly, drab; inquired; withering, dying

ℭℛ Nature Study

Birds See Winter Week 7 Nature Study Teaching Notes

ALL GLORY, LAUD, AND HONOR

All glory, laud, and honor,
To Thee, Redeemer, King,
To whom the lips of children
Made sweet hosannas ring!
Thou art the King of Israel,
Thou David's royal Son,
Who in the Lord's name comest,
The King and Blessèd One.

The people of the Hebrews
With palms before Thee went;
Our praise and prayer and anthems
Before Thee we present:
To Thee, before Thy passion,
They sang their hymns of praise;
To Thee, now high exalted,
Our melody we raise.

Thou didst accept their praises;
Accept the prayers we bring,
Who in all good delightest,
Thou good and gracious King!
All glory, laud, and honor
To Thee, Redeemer, King,
To whom the lips of children
Made sweet hosannas ring!

~ Theodulph of Orleans (translated by John Mason Neale)

◌ɞ SPELLING, GRAMMAR, AND WORD USAGE

Day 1 *Conjunctions & Commas*

Answer: Our praise, prayers, and anthems we present.

Sentence (example): All <u>glory</u> and <u>laud</u> and <u>honor</u> <u>are given</u> to the Lord. Jesus is called Redeemer, King, and Son. Jesus is called Redeemer and King and Son.

Day 2 *Rhyming Words*
Rhyming Words spelled the same: King - ring, went - present, praise - raise, bring - King

Rhyming Words spelled differently: Son - One,

Rhymes with sweet (will vary): tweet, repeat, meet, mete, suite

Rhymes with hymns: brims, whims, gyms, limbs

Day 3 *Subjects & Predicates*
Sentences (time expressions will vary): <u>Didst</u> Thou <u>accept</u> their praises? Do (Dost) You (Thou) now accept their praises? Will (Wilt) You (Thou) then accept their praises? The <u>children were singing</u> sweet hosannas. The child was singing sweet hosannas.

Proper nouns naming persons: Redeemer, King, King of Israel, David's royal Son, Hebrews, Lord's, Blessed One, children

Day 4 ~ *Homonyms, Synonyms, & Antonyms*
Homonyms: him, awl

Synonyms & antonyms (will vary): praise, adoration; reject; song; cruel, harsh

ℭℛ Nature Study
Birds See Winter Week 7 Nature Study Teaching Notes

THE GOOD SAMARITAN

But he, wanting to justify himself, said to Jesus, "And who is my neighbor?"

Then Jesus answered and said: "A certain man went down from Jerusalem to Jericho, and fell among thieves, who stripped him of his clothing, wounded him, and departed, leaving him half dead. Now by chance a certain priest came down that road. And when he saw him, he passed by on the other side. Likewise a Levite, when he arrived at the place, came and looked, and passed by on the other side. But a certain Samaritan, as he journeyed, came where he was. And when he saw him, he had compassion. So he went to him and bandaged his wounds, pouring on oil and wine; and he set him on his own animal, brought him to an inn, and took care of him. On the next day, when he departed, he took out two denarii, gave them to the innkeeper, and said to him, 'Take care of him; and whatever more you spend, when I come again, I will repay you.' So which of these three do you think was neighbor to him who fell among the thieves?"

And he said, "He who showed mercy on him."

Then Jesus said to him, "Go and do likewise."

~ Luke 10:29-37, New King James Version

℺ COPYBOOK & DICTATION

See *A Note About Scripture Copybook Selections* and *A Note About Names Referring to the Trinity* in the Copybook section of Pedagogy and Practice.

℺ SPELLING, GRAMMAR, AND WORD USAGE

Day 1 *Subjects & Predicates*

Sentences: Which <u>man</u> <u>is</u> neighbor? Which <u>man</u> <u>was</u> neighbor? Which man will be neighbor? A <u>Levite</u> <u>came</u> and looked. A Levite comes and looks. A Levite will come and look. (A Levite will come and will look.) Did thieves strip him of his clothing? Did a (the) thief strip him of his clothing? Parables teach truth. A (The) parable teaches truth.

Day 2 *Conjunctions & Commas*
Setnences: The thieves stripped him, wounded him, and departed. Is the priest or the Levite or the Samaritan the neighbor?

Day 3 *Suffix Review*
Answers: wanted, neighborly, clothes, bandaging, thieves, arriving, carelessness, mercies, saw, carefulness, mercifully, journeyed

Day 4 *Homonyms, Synonyms, & Antonyms*
Homonyms: bye, buy; whine

Synonyms & antonyms (will vary): hurt, injured, lacerated, harmed; arrive, come; lodge, tavern; cruelty, harshness, malice

CR NATURE STUDY
Birds See Winter Week 7 Nature Study Teaching Notes

PRIMER TWO SPRING TEACHING HELPS & NOTES

SPRING, WEEK 1

PIRATE STORY

Three of us afloat in the meadow by the swing,
Three of us aboard in the basket on the lea.
Winds are in the air, they are blowing in the spring,
And waves are on the meadow like the waves there are at sea.

Where shall we adventure, to-day that we're afloat,
Wary of the weather and steering by a star?
Shall it be to Africa, a-steering of the boat,
To Providence, or Babylon, or off to Malabar?

Hi! but here's a squadron a-rowing on the sea—
Cattle on the meadow a-charging with a roar!
Quick, and we'll escape them, they're as mad as they can be,
The wicket is the harbour and the garden is the shore.

~ Robert Louis Stevenson

℞ SPELLING, GRAMMAR, AND WORD USAGE

Remember that it is perfectly fine to help Primer students and prompt them with answers if they struggle.

Day 1 *Rhyming Words*

Rhyming words spelled the same: swing - spring, lea - sea, afloat - boat, star - Malabar

Rhyming words spelled differently: sea - be, roar - shore;

Rhyming words (may vary) - moat, gloat, wrote, throat; veer, cheer, near, spear, here, we're

Day 2 *Subjects & Predicates*

96

See Winter Teaching Helps & Notes, Week 7, for time expression ideas.

Sentences (time expressions will vary): <u>We</u> <u>shall escape</u> them. Now we escape them. We escaped them earlier. <u>Winds are blowing</u> in the spring. The wind is blowing in the spring.

Day 2 *Homonyms*
Homonyms: whether, sore

Day 3 *Noun Review*
Proper nouns that name places: Africa, Providence, Babylon, Malabar

Common nouns that name places: meadow, lea, sea, harbour, garden, shore

Common nouns that name things: swing, basket, waves, star, boat, squadron, cattle, wicket

Day 3 *Contractions*
Contractions: we're = we are; here's = here is; we'll = we shall (will)

Day 4 *Conjunctions & Commas*
Sentences (will vary): Shall we adventure to Africa, Providence, Babylon, or Malabar? Shall we adventure to Africa or Providence or Babylon or Malabar?

Day 4 *Simile*
Simile: waves on the meadow *are compared to* waves at sea

ℭℛ Nature Study

Review the instructions for Nature Study in the Pedagogy & Practice section of the Introduction.

The study of plants is called **botany**. Review the differences between plants and animals. What are the characteristics that plants and animals share? (*alive, growing, need nourishment, reproduce*) How are plants different from animals? (*plants generally stay in one spot; can make their own food; have no sensory organs - eyes, ears, etc.*) Animals and plants are dependent on each other in many ways. Plants help animals to live. They provide food, shelter, and clothing, among other things. Plants need carbon dioxide to produce their food, and in the process they give off oxygen. Animals need this oxygen to breathe, and in the process of respiration give off carbon dioxide, which plants need to produce their food. So the cycle goes. Help students appreciate this marvelous design.

This week, introduce Nature Study with these *Home Geography* lessons:

Lesson XIX: Useful Vegetables

Lesson XXX: Useful Grains

Lesson XXXI: Fruits

Lesson XXXII: Useful Plants

Lesson XXXIII: Forest Trees

Lesson XXXIV: Flowers

Lesson XXXV: Necessary to Make Plants Grow

As an ongoing project beginning this week, students are instructed to plant flower seeds. Each week, they will be prompted to observe the growth of the plants and sketch what they see in their nature notebooks.

To plant seeds, you will need:

* a small pot with a drainage hole at the bottom, and a saucer underneath
* some medium size rocks (driveway gravel works well)
* potting soil
* flower or vegetable seeds (choose ones with a quick germination time - check the package)

Before you plant the seeds, have students take a few seeds out of the package and draw a picture of them in their nature notebooks.

Put the rocks in the bottom third of the pot. This will allow water to drain but will keep the soil in. Fill the pot with dirt, leaving about 3/4 in. at the top. Take the seeds out of the package, and observe them. Look at the size, the shape, and the color. Are they hard or soft? If the seeds are larger, try cutting one open and observing.

Place a few of the remaining intact seeds on top of the soil, spacing them an inch or so apart. Press them into the soil to the depth indicated on the package. Then, water the seeds in the pot and place it in a sunny windowsill or on your back porch, if it is warm enough. Remember to water the growing plants a little each day, but be careful not to over-water. Most seed packages will have instructions for how to water and care for those particular seedlings.

In addition to observing and charting plant growth, students will conduct some simple experiments with the young plants over the next few weeks.

This week, students are instructed to study (or review) the parts of a flower. Use the links on the *Primer Resources Webpage* to find illustrations and explanations. Help students to identify and begin to learn the purpose of these plant flower parts: **stem, fruit, leaf, flower, seed, roots.** For the activity in the workbook, either have students draw and label the parts of the flower, or print out an illustration from one of the links and cut and paste it into the box on Day 2.

Beginning in Week 2, students will choose a plant each week to observe and study. Choose a flower which you can find in your backyard, in the park, along a trail, or in a meadow. Any flower will do, even those which some may consider a weed.

SPRING, WEEK 2

from RIKKI-TIKKI-TAVI

He was a mongoose, rather like a little cat in his fur and his tail, but quite like a weasel in his head and habits. His eyes and the end of his restless nose were pink; he could scratch himself anywhere he pleased, with any leg, front or back, that he chose to use; he could fluff up his tail till it looked like a bottle-brush, and his war-cry, as he scuttled through the long grass, was: 'Rikk-tikk-tikki-tikki-tchk!'

One day, a high summer flood washed him out of the burrow where he lived with his father and mother, and carried him, kicking and clucking, down a roadside ditch. He found a little wisp of grass floating there, and clung to it till he lost his senses. When he revived, he was lying in the hot sun on the middle of a garden path, very draggled indeed, and a small boy was saying: 'Here's a dead mongoose. Let's have a funeral.'

'No,' said his mother; 'let's take him in and dry him. Perhaps he isn't really dead.'

They took him into the house, and a big man picked him up between his finger and thumb, and said he was not dead but half choked; so they wrapped him in cotton-wool, and warmed him and he opened his eyes and sneezed.

~ *Jungle Book*, by Rudyard Kipling

ℂℛ COPYBOOK & DICTATION

Note that the first word of each paragraph of prose is indented. In typeset, you will sometimes see paragraphs that are not indented when they are separated by a line, as in this book. Show this to students, but always have them indent when they are writing by hand.

ℂℛ SPELLING, GRAMMAR, AND WORD USAGE

Day 1 *Adjectives ~ What Kind?*

Adjectives: little cat, restless nose, long grass, roadside ditch, little wisp, hot sun, small boy, big man, high summer flood

Day 2 *Adjectives ~ Which One? How Many?*

Work with students to make sure they understand that *a, an,* and *the* answer the adjective questions *which one?* and *how many?*

Adjetives: a mongoose, the end, any leg, a ditch, the sun, the middle, a path, a boy, a man

Day 2 *Simile*

Simile: mongoose's tail *is compared to* a bottle-brush

Students may suggest *like a little cat* and *like a weasel* as similes. Remind them that similes compare things which are not usually associated. Mongeese, cats, and weasels are all small mammals, so they do have a strong association.

Day 3 *Suffix Review*
Answers: littler; littlest; grasses; scuttling; reviving; revival; sneezy; enemies; draggle; pleasing; brushes; wrap; sensible; restlessness; mongeese, mongoose, or mongooses (*all are correct according to the* Oxford English Dictionary.)

Day 4 *Homonyms, Synonyms, & Antonyms*
Homonyms: fir, tale

Synonyms & antonyms (will vary): den, lair, tunnel; alive, living; rejuvenate, restore, rouse; calm, tranquil

ℭ NATURE STUDY
Choose a plant for study and observation each week. Talk with students and choose ones they would like to study. Co-op teachers may assign different flowers to individual students each week, and ask students to present their observations in the next class.

If you do not have immediate access to plants for observation, consider checking out books from the library or finding online resources to view and learn about specific flowers. Check the *Primer Resources Webpage* for links and resources to help with this.

The goal of these lessons is for students to simply observe a plant and talk about it with you. Review the parts of the plant they learned in Week 1, and then see if they can identify each one on their plant of the week, giving them plenty of help as needed. Do not worry if they cannot find all the parts or talk about every point listed; these are simply a guide to help the observation and discussion.

Students are also prompted to draw what is happening to their flower seeds each week.

The seed package should indicate how big the plants need to be before they are transplanted outdoors or into a bigger pot, and how far apart to plant the seedlings. Students can enjoy their plants for the entire summer.

Optional Enrichment Activities (see the *Primer Resources Webpage* for help with these activities):

* Learn new techniques, such as watercolor or chalk, for drawing or painting plants.
* Plan and plant a vegetable or flower garden.

SPRING, WEEK 3

PSALM 8

O Lord, our Lord,
  How excellent is Your name in all the earth,
Who have set Your glory above the heavens!
  Out of the mouth of babes and nursing infants
  You have ordained strength,
  Because of Your enemies,
  That You may silence the enemy and the avenger.

When I consider Your heavens, the work of Your fingers,
  The moon and the stars, which You have ordained,

What is man that You are mindful of him,
And the son of man that You visit him?

For You have made him a little lower than the angels,
And You have crowned him with glory and honor.
You have made him to have dominion over the works
of Your hands;
You have put all things under his feet,
All sheep and oxen—
Even the beasts of the field,
The birds of the air,
And the fish of the sea
That pass through the paths of the seas.

O Lord, our Lord,
How excellent is Your name in all the earth!

~ New King Janes Version

↷ COPYBOOK & DICTATION
See *A Note About Scripture Copybook Selections* and *A Note About Names Referring to the Trinity* in the Copybook section of Pedagogy and Practice.

↷ SPELLING, GRAMMAR, AND WORD USAGE
Day 1 *Adjective Elements: Possessive Forms*
Possessive Forms: our Lord, Your name, Your glory, Your enemies, Your fingers, his feet

Possessive Forms: their mouths, its path, my love, your songs, her words

Day 2 *Adjectives & Adjective Elements*

Adjectives (will vary): holy Lord, highest praise, little babes, the moon, many stars, a man, his son, bright angels, great honor, white sheep, my birds, vast seas, her name, whole earth

Day 3 *Suffixes: -ous, -ly, and -ful*

Answers: glorious, mindful, heavenly, lovely, adventurous, delightful, faithful, saintly, famous

Day 4 *Subjects & Predicates*

Verb tense answers (time expressions will vary): I consider Your heavens. Once upon a time, I considered Your heavens. I will consider Your heavens all the days of my life.

Singular/Plural answers: The enemy is silenced. The enemies are silenced. The sheep are His. The sheep are His.

ᛦ NATURE STUDY

Plants See Weeks 1-2 Spring Nature Study Teaching Notes.

SPRING, WEEK 4

from THE WIND IN THE WILLOWS

It all seemed too good to be true. Hither and thither through the meadows he rambled busily, along the hedgerows, across the copses, finding everywhere birds building, flowers budding, leaves thrusting—everything happy, and progressive, and occupied. And instead of having an uneasy conscience pricking him and whispering 'whitewash!' he somehow could only feel how jolly it was to be the only idle dog among all these busy citizens. After all, the best part of a holiday is perhaps not so much to be resting yourself, as to see all the other fellows busy working.

He thought his happiness was complete when, as he meandered aimlessly along, suddenly he stood by the edge of a full-fed river. Never in his life had he seen a river before—this sleek, sinuous, full-bodied animal, chasing and chuckling, gripping things with a gurgle and leaving them with a laugh, to fling itself on fresh playmates that shook themselves free, and were caught and held again. All was a-shake and a-shiver—glints and gleams and sparkles, rustle and swirl, chatter and bubble. The Mole was bewitched, entranced, fascinated. By the side of the river he trotted as one trots, when very small, by the side of a man who holds one spell-bound by exciting stories; and when tired at last, he sat on the bank, while the river still chattered on to him, a babbling procession of the best stories in the world, sent from the heart of the earth to be told at last to the insatiable sea.

~ Kenneth Grahame

℺ SPELLING, GRAMMAR, AND WORD USAGE
Day 1 *Adverbs Modifying Verbs*
Answers: Hither and thither *tells* where *he rambled;* busily *tells* how *he rambled.* Now *tells* when *he stood beside the river.* The Mole <u>was exhausted</u>. The Mole was finally exhausted. He <u>sat</u>. He sat down. The <u>river</u> <u>chattered</u>. The river chattered noisily.

Day 2 *Adverbs Modifying Adjectives*
Adverbs: The very happy <u>Mole</u> <u>stood</u> beside the river. Very modifies happy, *telling* to what extent.

Adverbs (modified adjectives will vary): more happy, very sleek, most insatiable, too idle, less busy, so fresh, least, quite jolly, really uneasy, not small.

Day 3 *Adverbs Modifying Other Adverbs*

Adverbs: He <u>rambled</u> so busily. (*So* is an adverb which modifies the adverb *busily*, which in turn modifies the verb *rambled. So* answers the question *to what extent?*

Adverbs (modified adverbs will vary): more sweetly, very gently, least quietly, too loudly, quite aimlessly, rather freely, always exuberantly, often happily.

Day 4 *Personification & Onomatopoeia*
Personification: river given characterstics of a living being - sleek, full-bodied, sinuous, having playmates; river given actions of a living being - chasing, chuckling, laughing, chattering, babbling

Onomatopoeia: chuckling, chattering, babbling

Day 4 *Homonyms, Synonyms, & Antonyms*
Homonyms: flour
Synonyms & antonyms (will vary): grove, thicket; purposefully, carefully; wander, ramble, traipse; released, dropped, freed

 CR NATURE STUDY
Plants See Weeks 1-2 Spring Nature Study Teaching Notes.

For this week's experiment, have students skip a watering or two and observe the effects. *Primer Two* students should also draw the plants on successive days in their nature notebooks as they observe.

SPRING, WEEK 5

ROCK OF AGES

Rock of Ages, cleft for me
Let me hide myself in thee;
Let the water and the blood,
From thy riven side which flowed,
Be of sin the double cure,
Cleanse me from its guilt and pow'r.

Not the labors of my hands
Can fulfil thy law's demands;
Could my zeal no respite know,
Could my tears forever flow,
All for sin could not atone;
Thou must save, and thou alone.

Nothing in my hand I bring,
Simply to thy cross I cling;
Naked, come to thee for dress,
Helpless, look to thee for grace;
Foul, I to the Fountain fly;
Wash me, Saviour, or I die.

While I draw this fleeting breath,
When mine eyelids close in death,
When I soar to worlds unknown,
See thee on thy judgment throne,
Rock of Ages, cleft for me,
Let me hide myself in thee.

~ Augustus Toplady

⊗ SPELLING, GRAMMAR, AND WORD USAGE
Day 1 *Adjectives, Adverbs, & Possessives*
Answers: the double cure, forever flow, could not atone, simply cling, thy riven side, my hands

Day 1 *Past Tense Forms*
Answers: cleft (cleaved), brought, knew

Day 2 *Rhyming Words*
Rhyming words spelled the same: hands - demands; know - flow; atone - alone; bring - cling, breath - death

Rhyming words spelled differently: me - thee; blood - flowed (slant rhyme); cure - pow'r (slant rhyme); dress - grace (slant rhyme); fly - die; unknown - throne; me - thee

Rhyming words (will vary): howl, scowl, towel, trowel

Day 3 *Suffixes: -ly*
Answers: doubly, simply, helplessly, helpfully, foully, fleetingly, softly, gracefully, suddenly

Day 4 *Subjects & Predicates*
Sentences: I cling to Thy cross. I clung to Thy cross. I will (shall) cling to Thy cross. I see Thee on Thy judgment throne. I saw Thee on Thy judgment throne. I will see Thee on Thy judgment throne. I am clinging to Thy cross. We are clinging to Thy cross.

CR NATURE STUDY
Plants See Weeks 1-2 Spring Nature Study Teaching Notes.

For this week's experiment, have students observe the stem. Does it grow straight up or does it lean or turn? Plants will usually turn toward the light. Do not tell students this, show them. Have them observe what happens when you turn the plant away from the light (*it should start leaning toward the light again*). *Primer Two* students should also draw what they observe in their nature notebooks.

SPRING, WEEK 6

from THE FALL OF TROY

At length, after a great deal of tugging and sweating by those at the ropes, the huge image began to move, the rollers beneath it creaked and groaned, and every Trojan shouted so loudly that the sound was heard far out to sea.

Slowly but steadily the multitude advanced across the plain, dragging the wonderful horse which they believed would bless the city. The sun had set before they passed through the breach in the wall; and the darkness of night was beginning to fall when the lumbering wheels ceased their noise. The great horse came to a standstill in a quiet corner close by the temple of Athene.

"My friends," said the king's officer, "we have done a fine day's work, and Athene's horse rests near the place where it shall remain. Now, indeed, the happiness of Troy is insured. Let every person depart to his own home; for tonight, the first time in ten years, we shall sleep in security, fearing no foe."

With joyful shouts and friendly goodnights the crowd separated, and every man went quietly to his own house. Soon the city was wrapped in darkness, and the streets were silent and empty. And Athene's horse stood grim and gaunt and motionless beside the temple wall.

~ *Thirty More Famous Stories Retold,* James Baldwin

❧ SPELLING, GRAMMAR, AND WORD USAGE

The English language makes extensive use of prepositions. Teaching students to quickly recognize prepositional phrases gives them a real advantage in analyzing sentences. Once all of the prepositional phrases in the sentence are identified, it is usually much easier to find the subject and the predicate, since a prepositional phrase can never be the subject or predicate.

In *Primer Two*, a primary goal is to memorize the list of common prepositions. See that students practice and review that list often.

Help the students understand how prepositions work in a sentence by demonstrating with this kinesthetic activity. You will need a small stuffed animal and a chair. Write on the whiteboard: *The bear is _ the chair*. Leave plenty of space to write in the appropriate preposition as you work through this exercise.

Ask students to place the bear under the chair. Fill in the blank on the whiteboard with the word *under*. Read the sentence and put parentheses around the prepositional phrase *under the chair*. Next, underline the subject *bear* and double underline the predicate *is*. Tell students that the preposition *under* relates the noun *chair* to the rest of the sentence. Discuss this, and then erase *under* from the sentence.

Next, ask students to place the bear in the chair, and fill in the blank with *in*. Again, read the sentence and put parentheses around the prepositional phrase *in the chair*. Tell students that the preposition *in* relates the noun *chair* to the rest of the sentence. Discuss this, and then erase *in* from the sentence.

Repeat this with as many prepositions as you have time for. Suggested prepositions: *above, against, before, behind, beside, beyond, near, over, underneath, upon*.

Demonstrate prepositions showing movement, such as *toward* and *away*. You will need to add words like *coming* or *going* so the sentence makes sense.

Come back to this activity often to help students grasp the concept. You can even have students position themselves to act out the prepositions—be creative!

Day 1 *Prepositions*
Sentences: The <u>multitude</u> <u>advanced</u> across the plain. Every <u>man</u> <u>went</u> to his own house.

Day 2 *Adjectives, Adverbs, & Possessives*
Answers: the huge image, friendly goodnights, shouted loudly, so loudly, fine day's work, Athene's horse

Day 2 *Personification & Onomatopoeia*
Personfication: The horse is given the human characteristic of grimness.

Onomatopoeia: creaked, groaned

Day 3 *Suffixes: -er and -est*
Comparatives: louder, loudest; quieter, quietest; closer, closest; steadier, steadiest; darker, darkest; grimmer, grimmest

Day 4 *Homonyms, Synonyms, & Antonyms*
Homonyms: see, past

Synonyms & antonyms (will vary): finish, end, quit; loud, noisy, clamorous; thin, dismal, dreary; friend, ally

ᘏ Nature Study
Weather and Winds In bygone days, men and women who kept journals often noted the weather each day. When

there was no air conditioning or heat, and certainly when life and livelihood depended on agriculture, the weather was a constant source of interest and concern.

For the next month, students should make note of the weather and wind direction each day. Help students construct a calendar in their nature notebooks on two facing pages with blanks large enough to make note of weather and wind through the month. Alternately, a blank calendar for this purpose is included in the Appendix of *Primer Two Spring*. Copy it on cardstock and have students keep it out where they will see it and be reminded.

Introduce nature study this week with *Home Geography*:

Lesson VI: What the Wind Brings

Wind direction tells in which direction the wind originates. In other words, FROM WHICH DIRECTION is the wind blowing? A very simple way to determine the wind direction is to use bubbles. Go outside, blow bubbles, and observe which way they are blown in relation to your house. If they are not blown at all, the winds are said to be calm. Wind direction and weather conditions can change during the day, so note the time of day when you record the weather and wind information.

Decide together with students how to record the weather and wind information, and any additional information to be recorded on their weather charts. Some suggestions:

+ Sunny, cloudy, or rainy? Draw symbols for each.

+ If you have a thermometer, record the

113

temperature each morning, or any time of day.
Try to record at the same time each day.

• Types of clouds seen in the sky.

For this week's lesson, review the different types of clouds.
There are links on the *Primer Resources Webpage* to websites
with excellent illustrations and explanations. Have students
draw and label the four cloud types listed.

SPRING, WEEK 7

from THE BROOK

I come from haunts of coot and hern,
I make a sudden sally,
And sparkle out among the fern,
To bicker down a valley.

By thirty hills I hurry down,
Or slip between the ridges,
By twenty thorps, a little town,
And half a hundred bridges.

Till last by Philip's farm I flow
To join the brimming river,
For men may come and men may go,
But I go on forever.

I chatter over stony ways,
In little sharps and trebles,
I bubble into eddying bays,
I babble on the pebbles.

With many a curve my banks I fret
By many a field and fallow,
And many a fairy foreland set

With willow-weed and mallow.

I chatter, chatter, as I flow
To join the brimming river,
For men may come and men may go,
But I go on forever.

~Alfred, Lord Tennyson

◯ȝ SPELLING, GRAMMAR, AND WORD USAGE

Day 1 Prepositions

Prepositions: between the ridges, over stony ways, into eddying bays, on the pebbles, with many a curve, of coot and hern, in little sharps and trebles, with willow-weed and mallow

Day 2 Adjectives, Adverbs, & Possessives

Answers: thirty hills, hurry down, Philip's farm, go on forever

Day 3 Rhyming Words

Rhyming words spelled the same: hern - fern; down - town; ridges - bridges; ways - bays; fret - set; fallow - mallow;

Rhyming words spelled differently: sally - valley; flow - go; river - forever (slant rhyme); trebles - pebbles

Rhyming with curve *(will vary):* nerve, swerve, reserve;

Rhyming with field *(will vary):* shield, yield, healed, sealed, peeled, wheeled

Day 4 Alliteration, Personification, & Onomatopoeia

Other alliteration in the selection: haunts of coot and hern; thirty hills I hurry down; twenty thorps, a little town; half a hundred bridges; men may come and men may go; my banks I fret by many a field and fallow; with willow-weed

115

Personification: The entire poem is a personification of the brook, which speaks in the first person. The brook is also given human actions: *make, bicker, hurry, slip, chatter, fret.*

Onomatopoeia: chatter, babble

ℂℜ NATURE STUDY

Learn about the water cycle—just one of many evidences that the world is intricately designed for our comfort and delight. See the links on the *Primer Resources Webpage* for explanations and illustrations.

For the activity, draw a simplified scheme of the water cycle on the whiteboard for the students to copy.

SPRING, WEEK 8

From THE SECRET GARDEN

Colin saw it all, watching each change as it took place. Every morning he was brought out and every hour of each day when it didn't rain he spent in the garden. Even gray days pleased him. He would lie on the grass "watching things growing," he said. If you watched long enough, he declared, you could see buds unsheath themselves. Also you could make the acquaintance of strange busy insect things running about on various unknown but evidently serious errands, sometimes carrying tiny scraps of straw or feather or food, or climbing blades of grass as if they were trees from whose tops one could look out to explore the country. A mole throwing up its mound at the end of its burrow and making its way out at last with the long-nailed paws which looked so like elfish hands, had absorbed him one whole morning. Ants' ways, beetles' ways, bees' ways, frogs' ways, birds' ways, plants' ways, gave him a new world to explore and when Dickon revealed them all and added foxes' ways, otters' ways, ferrets' ways, squirrels' ways, and trout's and water-rats' and badgers' ways, there was no end to the things to talk about and think over.

And this was not the half of the Magic. The fact that he had really once stood on his feet had set Colin thinking tremendously and when Mary told him of the spell she had worked he was excited and approved of it greatly. He talked of it constantly.

"Of course there must be lots of Magic in the world," he said wisely one day, "but people don't know what it is like or how to make it. Perhaps the beginning is just to say nice things are going to happen until you make them happen. I am going to try and experiment."

~ Frances Hodgson Burnett

ℭ Spelling, Grammar, and Word Usage

Alert students may notice in the series of possessive nouns followed by the word *ways*, that the word *trout* is the only possessive in the series that doesn't end with an **-s.** Ask them why this is so? (Trout *is both the singular form and the plural form. Review other words like this:* sheep, dust, mongoose, *etc.*)

Day 1 *Prepositions*
Prepositions: in the garden, on the grass, of straw or feather or food, on his feet, of it

Day 1 *Homonyms*
Homonyms: reign, rein; pause; weigh, whey

Day 2 , *Adjectives, Adverbs, & Possessives*
Answers: strange busy insect things, evidently serious, thinking tremendously

117

Possessive (may vary): bees' ways

Day 2 , Book Titles
Note that underlining book titles is generally only used when writing by hand. When typing a book title, it is usually italicized instead.

Day 3 Conjunctions & Commas
Sentences (will vary): Colin spent his days in the garden watching plants grow, watching insects scurry, or watching animals play. Colin spent his days in the garden watching plants grow or watching insects scurry or watching animals play.

Day 4 Comparison with more, less, most and least
Comparitives: rainier, rainiest; less serious, least serious; more tremendously, most tremendously; more constantly, most constantly; less wisely, least wisely

CR NATURE STUDY
Insects are fascinating creatures, fun to watch and full of wonderful lessons for our lives. Although some insects are harmful to man, almost all insects have some specific purpose in our world. (I must admit I am still waiting to find out the purpose of mosquitos and ticks—both of which abound in Virginia!)

There are a few tools which, though not required, will make the collection and observation of insects a bit easier. Among the most helpful are a bug viewer with a magnifying lens and a butterfly net. See the links on the *Primer Resources Webpage* for inexpensive versions of these. You will no doubt be able to find many books with fascinating information and pictures at your local library.

Do not neglect the practice of simply going outside and watching a bug. It is amazing how very still a normally wiggly student can sit while watching a busy ant carrying food. Caution students not to touch insects, as many will bite and some are poisonous.

Insects Review the characteristics of an insect (from *Primer One Spring*.)

✓ ***Insects do not have a backbone, but have an* exoskeleton.** **Exo-** means *oustide*—the skeleton of an insect is outside of its body. Because insects do not have backbones, they are called **invertebrates.** Discuss with students how insects differ from fish, mammals, birds, and reptiles, all of which have backbones.

✓ ***Insects have three main body parts:* head, thorax, and abdomen.** Find a picture illustrating this, either in a book or from the field guide link on the *Primer Resources Webpage.*

✓ ***Insects have a pair of* antennae on their heads.** *Antennae* is plural; the singular form is *antenna.*

✓ ***Insects have three pairs of legs.***

✓ ***Insects have two pairs of wings.***

Examples of insects include: *fly, mosquito, tick, ant, grasshopper, bee, wasp, dragonfly, gnat, flea, cricket, butterfly, praying mantis,* and *moth.*

Spiders Introduce the characteristics of the spider to students

119

and compare them with those of the insect. Find a picture illustrating these characteristics in a book or on the field guide link from the *Primer Resources Webpage*. Compare spiders with insects.

	Spider	**Insect**
Vertebrate or invertebrate?	invertebrate	invertebrate
Body parts	2	3
Legs?	4 pairs	3 pairs
Eyes?	8 eyes	2 eyes
Wings?	no	may have
Antennae?	no	yes

Spiders are classified as **arachnids.** This name comes from the Greek story of the mortal Arachne, who foolishly boasted that she could spin more beautifully than the goddess Athena. Read the story of *The Wonderful Weaver*, linked from the *Primer Resources Webpage*.

SPRING, WEEK 9

From THE STORY-BOOK OF SCIENCE

To weave its web, each kind of spider has its own method

of procedure, according to the kind of game it is going to hunt, the places it frequents, and according to its particular inclinations, tastes, and instincts. I will merely tell you a few words about the epeirae, large spiders magnificently speckled with yellow, black, and silvery white. They are hunters of big game, — of green or blue damsel-flies that frequent the water-courses, of butterflies, and large flies. They stretch their web vertically between two trees and even from one bank of a stream to the other. Let us examine this last case.

An epeira has found a good place for hunting: the dragon-flies, or blue and green damsel-flies, come and go from one tuft of reeds to another, some times going up, sometimes down the stream. Along its course are butterflies also, and horse-flies, or large flies that suck blood from cattle. The site is a good one. Now, then, to work! The epeira climbs to the top of a willow at the water's edge.

With its hind legs it draws a thread from its spinnerets. The thread lengthens and lengthens; it floats from the top of the branch. The spider draws out more and more; finally, it stops. Is the thread long enough? Is it too short? That is what must be looked after. If too long, it would be wasting the precious silky liquid; if too short, it would not fulfil the given conditions. A glance is thrown at the distance to be crossed, an exact glance, you may be sure. The thread is found too short. The spider lengthens it by drawing out a little more. Now all goes well: the thread has the wished-for length, and the work is done. The epeira waits at the top of its branch: the rest will be accomplished without help. From time to time it bears with its legs on the thread to see if it resists. Ah! it resists; the bridge is fixed! The spider crosses the stream on its suspension bridge! What has happened, then? This: The thread floated from the top of the willow. A breath of air blew the free end of the thread into the branches on the opposite bank. This end got entangled there; behold the mystery. The epeira has only to draw the thread to itself, to stretch it properly and make a suspension bridge of it.

~Jean-Henri Fabre

ℭ Spelling, Grammar, and Word Usage

Day 1 Interjections

Interjection: Hi! but here's a squadron a-rowing on the sea, Cattle on the meadow a-charging with a roar! ("Pirate Story" by Robert Louis Stevenson)

Day 1 Conjunctions & Commas

Sentences (will vary): The thread floated from the willow, across the string, and onto the branch. The thread floated from the willow and across the string and onto the branch.

Day 2 Comparison ~ Irregular Forms

Students will probably require help with this activity.

Answers: bad, worse, worst; little, less, least; much, more, most; many, more, most; far, farther, farthest

Day 3 Prepositions, Adjectives, Adverbs, & Possessives

Answers: down the stream, from its spinnerets, precious silky liquid, this last case, stretch vertically, too long, goes well, water's edge, its suspension bridge

Day 4 Plural Forms Ending in -ae

Plural Forms: antennae; larvae; vertebrae

ℭ Nature Study

Each week, students are directed to choose a spider to observe, discuss, and draw. Students are asked to observe and draw the spider's web. As always, it is best to have students observe and identify the actual spiders which live in your geographical area if at all possible. Remind students not to touch spiders. Make sure that students can recognize the poisonous spiders that live in your area as a saftely precaution. As needed, use field guides, books, and online resources to study, observe, and identify. See the links on the *Primer Resources Webpage.*

THE BEATITUDES

Blessed are the poor in spirit, for theirs is the kingdom of heaven.

Blessed are those who mourn, for they shall be comforted.

Blessed are the meek, for they shall inherit the earth.

Blessed are those who hunger and thirst for righteousness, for they shall be filled.

Blessed are the merciful, for they shall obtain mercy.

Blessed are the pure in heart, for they shall see God.

Blessed are the peacemakers, for they shall be called sons of God.

Blessed are those who are persecuted for righteousness' sake, for theirs is the kingdom of heaven.

Blessed are you when they revile and persecute you, and say all kinds of evil against you falsely for My sake. Rejoice and be exceedingly glad, for great is your reward in heaven, for so they persecuted the prophets who were before you.

~ Matthew 5:3-12, New King James Version

ℭ COPYBOOK & DICTATION

See *A Note About Scripture Copybook Selections* and *A Note About Names Referring to the Trinity* in the Copybook section of Pedagogy and Practice.

ℭ SPELLING, GRAMMAR, AND WORD USAGE

Day 1 *Prepositions, Adjectives, Adverbs, & Possessives*

Prepositions: against you, before you, so persecuted, exceedingly glad, say falsely, righteousness' sake, My sake

Day 2 *Word Usage ~ Forms of Comparison*

Sentences: Your reward in heaven is greater. Your reward in heaven is greatest. God shall be more merciful. God shall be most merciful. Christians do well to suffer with patience, because God promises us a good reward. It is good to suffer with patience becuase God promises to reward us well.

Day 3 *Subjects & Predicates*

Sentences: <u>They</u> <u>hunger</u> and <u>thirst</u> for righteousness. They hungered and thirsted for righteousness. They shall hunger and (shall) thirst for righteousness. The meek <u>shall inherit</u> the earth. The meek inherit the earth. The meek inherited the earth. The prophets <u>were persecuted</u> before you. The prophet was persecuted before you. <u>They</u> <u>revile</u> and <u>persecute</u> you. He reviles and persecutes you.

Day 4 *Pronouns: Possessive* **Your** *Homonyms*

Possessives: You're going to receive your reward in heaven.

❧ NATURE STUDY

Spiders See Weeks 8-9 Spring Nature Study Teaching Notes.

from SPEECH TO THE VIRGINIA CONVENTION

Sir, we are not weak if we make a proper use of those means which the God of nature hath placed in our power. The millions of people, armed in the holy cause of liberty, and in such a country as that which we possess, are invincible by any force which our enemy can send against us. Besides, Sir, we shall not fight our battles alone. There is a just God who presides over the destinies of nations, and who will raise up friends to fight our battles for us. The battle, Sir, is not to the strong alone; it is to the vigilant, the active, the brave. Besides, Sir, we have no election. If we were base enough to desire it, it is now too late to retire from the contest. There is no retreat but in submission and slavery! Our chains are forged! Their clanking may be heard on the plains of Boston! The war is inevitable~and let it come! I repeat it, Sir, let it come.

It is in vain, Sir, to extentuate the matter. Gentlemen may cry, Peace, Peace~but there is no peace. The war is actually begun! The next gale that sweeps from the north will bring to our ears the clash of resounding arms! Our brethren are already in the field! Why stand we here idle? What is it that gentlemen wish? What would they have? Is life so dear, or peace so sweet, as to be purchased at the price of chains and slavery? Forbid it, Almighty God! I know not what course others may take; but as for me, give me liberty or give me death!

~ Patrick Henry, on March 20, 1775 at St. John's Church

♋ SPELLING, GRAMMAR, AND WORD USAGE
Day 1 *Prepositions, Adjectives, Adverbs, & Possessives*
Answers: against us, on the plains, of chains and slavery, the holy cause, a just God, too late, so dear, know not, our chains

Day 2 *Conjunctions & Commas*
Answers: The battle is to the vigilant, to the active, and to the brave. The battle is to the vigilant and to the active and to the brave.

125

Day 2 *Alliteration & Onomatopoeia*
Alliteration: . . . hath p̲laced in our p̲ower...who will raise up friends to f̲ight our battles f̲or us . . . is p̲eace s̲o s̲weet as to be p̲urchased at the p̲rice of chains and s̲lavery?

Onomatopoeia: clanking, clash

Day 3 *Homonyms, Synonyms, & Antonyms*
Homonyms: week; vane, vein; deer

Synonyms & antonyms (will vary): freedom; careless, heedless, inattentive; allies; cowardly, fearful

Day 4 *Pronouns ~ Possessive* Their *& Homonyms*
Answer: They're hearing their clanging on the plains there in Boston.

ॐ Nature Study
Spiders See Weeks 8-9 Spring Nature Study Teaching Notes.

Spring, Week 12 _____

ETERNAL FATHER, STRONG TO SAVE

Eternal Father, strong to save,
Whose arm hath bound the restless wave,
Who bidd'st the mighty ocean deep
Its own appointed limits keep;
Oh, hear us when we cry to Thee,
For those in peril on the sea!

O Christ! Whose voice the waters heard
And hushed their raging at Thy word,

Who walked'st on the foaming deep,
And calm amidst its rage didst sleep;
Oh, hear us when we cry to Thee,
For those in peril on the sea!

Most Holy Spirit! Who didst brood
Upon the chaos dark and rude,
And bid its angry tumult cease,
And give, for wild confusion, peace;
Oh, hear us when we cry to Thee,
For those in peril on the sea!

O Trinity of love and power!
Our brethren shield in danger's hour;
From rock and tempest, fire and foe,
Protect them wheresoe'er they go;
Thus evermore shall rise to Thee
Glad hymns of praise from land and sea.

~ William Whiting

☞ COPYBOOK & DICTATION

See *A Note About Names Referring to the Trinity* in the Copybook section of Pedagogy and Practice.

Explain the words which are written with missing letters: *bidds't walkeds't,* and *wheresoe'er.* It is a frequently used convention in poetry to shorten words, leaving out letters or replacing them with an apostrophe, in order to create or to keep a certain meter. The technical term for this is *elision.* Encourage students look for other examples of this in a poetry book.

☞ SPELLING, GRAMMAR, AND WORD USAGE
Day 1 *Prepositions, Adjectives, Adverbs, & Possessives*
Answers: amidst its rage, upon the chaos, to Thee, mighty

ocean deep, chaos dark and rude, calm didst sleep, evermore shall rise, its own appointed limits, danger's hour

Day 2 *Rhyming Words*:
Rhyming words spelled the same: save - wave; deep - keep; deep - sleep

Rhyming words spelled differently: Thee - sea; heard - word; brood - rude; cease - peace; power - hour; foe - go

Rhyming words (will vary): fight, flight, bite, site, byte

Day 3 *Conjunctions & Commas*
Answers (will vary): We shall be safe from rock, from tempest, from fire, or from foe. We shall be safe from rock or from tempest or from fire or from foe.

Day 3 *Pronouns* ~ *Possessive* its *Homonyms*
Answers: Tell the chaos it's time to cease its angry tumult.

Day 4 *Alliteration & Personification*
Alliteration: Strong to save; From rock and tempest, fire and foe;

Personification: Waves, ocean, waters, and chaos are given human characteristics or actions.

ⓒ NATURE STUDY
Spiders See Weeks 8-9 Spring Nature Study Teaching Notes.

APPENDIX

The phonics and spelling rules reviewed in *Primer Two* are listed below, along with the lesson(s) where these rules are reviewed. This is not intended to be an exhaustive list of rules, nor are they introduced in any particular order, but are introduced as they occur in literary selections. It is expected that all Primer students are concurrently studying a comprhensive phonics and spelling course.

LETTER & PHONOGRAM SOUNDS

♦ Words ending in the soft sound of **c** or **g** often end with a silent **e**. The letter **c** always says /s/ before **e, i,** or **y**. The letter **g** may say /j/ before **e, i,** or **y**. The silent **e** at the end of the word indicates that the **c** or the **g** says its soft sound. *(Winter Week 2)*

SPELLING RULES & TIPS

♦ Use **i** before **e**, except after **c**, and when it says /ā/ as in *neighbor*. There are a few exceptions which should be memorized: *either, neither, height, seize, leisure, foreign, sovereign, counterfeit, protein, weird (Autumn Weeks 3 & 10, Winter Week 4)*.

♦ Make most names of persons, places, things, or ideas plural (more than one) by adding **-s** or **-es** to the base word. *(Autumn Week 1)*

Words that end a single vowel **y** (not a vowel digraph like **-ay, -ey,** or **-oy**), change the **y** to an **i** and add **-es**. Example: puppy, change y → i + es = puppies. *(Autumn Weeks 1 & 2, Winter Week 10, Spring Weeks 1 & 2)*

In some words ending in **f**, the **f** changes to **v** and then you add **-es**. Example: leaf, change f → v + es = leaves. Some words have an internal change, like *mice*, and some words have no change at all, like *dust*. *(Autumn, Week 5)*

* Some English words ending in **-a**, derived from Latin, are made plural by changing the **-a** to **-ae**. Example: *antenna* → *antennae* *(Spring Week 9)*

* The suffix indicating the past tense is **-ed**. It says /d/ or /t/ unless the base word ends in **-d** or **-t**, in which case it says /**ed**/. Sometimes the past tense is formed by totally changing the word. Example: *have* → *had* *(Autumn, Week 2, Winter Week 3, Spring Week 2)*

* To add a suffix that begins with a vowel to a one-syllable word, double the final consonant IF the word ends in one vowel followed by one consonant that you can see AND hear. *(Autumn Week 9)*

* To add a suffix that begins with a vowel to a two-syllable word, double the final consonant if the base word ends in one vowel then one consonant that you can see AND hear, and the accent is on the last syllable of the base word. *(Autumn Week 10, Winter Week 4)*

* Words that end with a silent **e** drop the **e** when a suffix that begins with a vowel is added, unless dropping the **e** interferes with another spelling rule. *(Autumn Week 7, Winter Week 2)*

* When *full* is added to another word to make a new compound word, it is spelled with just one **l**. *(Autumn Week 8)*

* An **apostrophe (')** + s is added to a word to show possession. *(Autumn Week 4)*

- To form the possessive of plural words ending in **-s**, add the **apostrophe (')** alone after the **-s**. *(Autumn Week 6)*

  Some words ending in **-s** make the possessive form by just adding an **apostrophe (')** alone after the **-s**. Example: *righteousness'* *(Spring Week 10)*

- A **contraction** shortens a group of words by replacing a letter or letters with an **apostrophe (')**. *(Winter Week 5)*

Grammar & Word Usage

- **Homonyms** are words that sound the same, but have different spellings and meanings. *Dear* and *deer* are homonyms. *(Autumn Week 2, Winter Week 1, Spring Week 1)*

- **Synonyms** are words that have similar meanings, like *happy* and *glad*. *(Autumn Week 2, Winter Week 1, Spring Week 2)*

- **Antonyms** are words that have opposite meanings, like *happy* and *sad*. *(Autumn Week 3, Winter Week 1, Spring Week 2)*

- When a noun names only one person, place, thing, or idea, it is said to be **singular**. When it names two or more, it is **plural**. *(Autumn Week 4, Winter Week 1)*

- A noun that names a particular one person, place, thing, or idea is said to be a **proper noun**. A noun that is common to a group of persons, places, things, or ideas is said to be a **common noun**. *(Autumn Week 5, Winter Week 1, Spring Week 1)*

- Proper nouns begin with a capital letter. *(Autumn Week 5)*

- The first letter of a title used as part of a name is capitalized. Titles are often abbreviated. *(Autumn Week 6)*

* A **pronoun** is a word that stands in for a noun. *(Autumn Week 7)*

* **Possessive pronouns** NEVER use an apostrophe. *(Autumn Week 7, Winter Week 1, Spring Week 3)*

  Possessive pronoun **its** has a homonym: **it's,** which is the contraction for *it is. (Autumn Week 7, Spring Week 12)*

  Possessive pronoun **your** has a homonym: **you're,** which is the contraction for *you are. (Autumn Week 12, Spring Week 10)*

  Possessive pronoun **whose** has a homonym: **who's,** which is the contraction for *who is. (Autumn Week 12)*

  Possessive pronoun **their** has two homonyms: **there** and **they're,** which is the contraction for *they are. (Spring Week 10)*

* A **verb** is a word that shows action, being, or state. *(Winter Week 2)*

* **Verbs** have the property of **tense,** that indicates when the action, being, or state occurred. **Present tense** indicates that the action, being, or state is occurring now, **past tense** indicates that it happened before now, and **future tense** indicates that it will happen after now. *(Winter Week 3)*

* A verb telling the action, being, or state of a singular noun or pronoun is said to be **singular.** A verb telling the action, being, state of two or more, is said to be **plural.** Many verbs change form to show whether they are singular or plural. *(Winter Week 4)*

* A **sentence** begins with a capital letter, ends with end punctuation, and expresses a complete thought. *(Spring Week 1)*

* The **subject** of a sentence tells who or what the sentence

is about. The **predicate** tells what the subject is or does. (*Winter Week 5*)

* In some sentences, such as lines of poetry or sentences that ask a question, the predicate verb may precede the subject.

* When the subject of a sentence is *I* or *we*, the verb *shall* is generally used. *Will* is properly used only to show strong determination. (*Winter Week 6*)

* **Conjunctions** joins words or groups of words. (*Winter Week 8, Spring Week 1*)

* Sentences with words or groups of words in a series usually use a comma between each item of the series, and a comma and a conjunction before the final item. (*Winter Week 11, Spring Week 8*)

* An **adjective** is a word that modifies a noun or a pronoun, answering the questions *what kind? which one?* or *how many?* (*Winter Week 2*)

* **Possessive nouns** and **pronouns** are **adjective elements** answering the question *whose?* (*Winter Week 2*)

* Adding the suffixes **-ous, -ful,** and **-y** can transform a noun into an adjective. (*Spring Week 3*)

* An **adverb** is a word that modifies a verb, an adjective or another adverb, answering the questions *where? when? why? how?* or *to what extent?* (*Winter Week 2*)

* Adding the suffix **-ly** can transform a word into an adverb. (*Spring Week 6*)

* The suffixes **-er** and **-est** are often added to adverbs and adjectives to show a degree of comparison (*Spring Week 6*)

Words with two or more syllables may use the adverbs more or most, or less or least, before the word to show comparison. *(Spring Week 8)*

Some words change completely to show comparison, such as good → better → best. *(Spring Week 9)*

- Good is an adjective, and should be used only to modify a noun or pronoun. *Well* is an adverb, and should be used to modify a verb, adjective, or adverb answering the questions *how?* or *to what extent?* *(Spring Week 9)*

- A **preposition** is a word that modifies a verb, an adjective or another adverb, answering the questions *where? when? why? how? to what extent?* or *(Winter Week 2)*

- Enclose poems and song titles with quotation marks and capitalize all of the important words. *(Spring Week 7)*

- Underline book titles and capitalize all of the important words. *(Spring Week 7)*

- An **interjection** is a word that shows sudden or strong emotion. *(Spring Week 9)*

FIGURES OF SPEECH

- A **simile** compares two things that are not usually associated with one another by using the words *like, as,* or *than.* *(Autumn Week 4, Winter Week 7, Spring Week 8)*

- In **onomatopoeia,** the spelling or sound of a word gives a clue to its meaning. Sometimes it is an imitation of a particular sound, such as *oink* or *splash.* *(Autumn Week 11, Winter Week 5, Spring Week 4)*

- **Personification** gives qualities of living things to inanimate objects or human characteristics to non-humans. *(Winter Weeks 2 & 9, Spring Week 4)*

• In **alliteration,** the beginning sounds of words close to each other are repeated. *(Spring Week 7)*

BEGINNING CONSONANT BLENDS FOR RHYMING

th, sh, ch, wh, pr, tr, gr, br, cr, dr, fr, st, sp, sk, sc, sw, sm, sn, pl, cl, bl, fl, sl, gl, tw, str, spl, spr

NOTES

Made in the USA
Lexington, KY
20 March 2018